THE PURSUIT OF IDEALS

Publication Number 787

AMERICAN LECTURE SERIES®

A Monograph in

AMERICAN LECTURES IN PHILOSOPHY

Edited by

MARVIN FARBER, Ph.D.

Department of Philosophy

State University of New York at Buffalo

THE PURSUIT OF IDEALS

By

YERVANT H. KRIKORIAN

Professor of Philosophy, Emeritus
The City College of the City University of New York

CHARLES C THOMAS • PUBLISHER
Springfield · Illinois · U.S.A.

Published and Distributed Throughout the World by

CHARLES C THOMAS • PUBLISHER

BANNERSTONE HOUSE

301-327 East Lawrence Avenue, Springfield, Illinois, U.S.A.

NATCHEZ PLANTATION HOUSE

735 North Atlantic Boulevard, Fort Lauderdale, Florida, U.S.A.

With THOMAS BOOKS *careful attention is given to all details of manufacturing and design. It is the Publisher's desire to present books that are satisfactory as to their physical qualities and artistic possibilities and appropriate for their particular use.* THOMAS BOOKS *will be true to those laws of quality that assure a good name and good will.*

Printed in the United States of America

E-1

To
Kathleen Jean Rogers
for her essence and existence

PREFACE

The present era despite its high sophistication is an era of violent conflicts between ideals, as between conservatism and liberalism or new-leftism to cite only the widespread difference in political ideals. Basic commitments in politics, morality, religion, and in all other areas have their roots in ideals and future hopes. Most of our activities are concerned with immediate, everyday attainable objectives; yet the pursuit of approachable though not fully attainable ideals is a necessary condition for a meaningful, satisfactory life.

The philosophic framework of the present discussion is melioristic and naturalistic; it is melioristic in the sense that it is hopeful, with faith in human intelligence and effort as a means of progressively realizing ideal possibilities; it is naturalistic in the sense that whatever we know is part of the complex forces and events of nature; and the method of approach will be critical as well as descriptive. The ideals that have been chosen for discussion are those that are necessary for human fulfillment. These will be the ideals of pure and technological science, of morality, and of art, which taken together will constitute religion. One must not pretend, of course, to an expert's knowledge in all these fields, but the issues involved are not limited to experts since they concern us all. And in further defence of so comprehensive a venture it should be pointed out that, however tentative or unfinished the result may be, this attempt is desirable in a culture that is fragmented by too much emphasis on specialization.

I have used some material, though with considerable modification, from an essay of mine in *Naturalism and the Human Spirit* and from two of my articles in *Ararat*. The present discussion, however, has its own unity and coherence.

I wish to thank three friends who have been most helpful in this project, Christopher B. Garnett, Jr., August R. Leisner, and Vahan Sewny. I owe especially much to Vahan Sewny with whom I have had hours of discussion and whose numerous suggestions have been incorporated into my analysis.

CONTENTS

CONTENTS

THE PURSUIT OF IDEALS

Chapter I

INTRODUCTION

From time immemorial human beings have been concerned with finding the conditions for a successful, satisfying way of life. Many thoughtful solutions have been suggested, but none seems to have gained universal assent. Despite the failures, this problem cannot be ignored. Though no answer can claim finality, the very urge of life demands a guiding direction.

I

The answers given to this question have been many and varied, some other-worldly and some this-worldly.

The other-worldly answers, especially those of the Judeo-Christian tradition, find the ultimate satisfaction of life in doing the will of God. "If a man really abides in God's will," says the devout Meister Eckhart, "even the pains of hell would be a joy to him." This and many similar precepts have declared the same message. To find God's will, some religious traditions resort to God's written and unwritten Laws, others to the authority of the Church, *extra ecclesiam solus non est,* still others to the inner conscience of the individual, and the mystics resort to their vision of God. God as the ultimate expression of love, justice, righteousness, and power has been a source of inspiration to many worshippers. As love, He has inspired human beings to love one another; as justice and righteousness, He has furthered decent human relations; as power, He has given a sense of security and of final triumph.

And yet the other-worldly way of human fulfillment has its dangers: in transferring human aspirations and the sources of power to a supernatural realm, the natural world has often been demeaned. In its extreme form this transference has resulted in asceticism which by condemning the flesh and natural desires brought a divisive conflict into human nature. Instead of seeking the roots of human aspirations in one's natural existence, this way of fulfillment has wandered into extranatural worlds. And, again, instead of facing the difficulties of life with maximum courage and intelligence, it has drifted into imaginary sources to get power. The other-worldly percepts to attain human satisfaction have no longer any appeal to the modern mind. The very values attributed to a supernatural Being have their abode and reality in the natural world, and they can flourish without the other-worldly premises. The precepts, on the other hand, are based on authority, on unverifiable revelations, and in inaccessible experience. The kind of satisfaction the modern mind looks for must be found in this world without imaginary support from some other world.

Of the this-worldly reflections on human fulfillment some are realistically oriented, that is, reality is conceived as physical, economic, and political force or power; others give expression to disillusionment, finding no way to satisfaction; and still others are hopeful, with faith in human effort as a means of realizing ideal possibilities.

The realist is the one who is usually not guided by utopian ideals, but by what he claims to be realities. And these realities are taken to be power, self-interest, political dominance, and material profits. The realistically enlightened and thus supposed to be free of illusions, and their pursuit of happiness is believed to be rooted in the substantial aspects of existence. What counts most for the realist is observable, material success, and for this success any means is permissible.

The conflict between the realist and the imaginative idealist is usually between what exists or is firmly established and what ought to be to satisfy the needs of the principled individual. The realist is inclined to feel superior to the idealist, demeaning his enthusiasm for ideals and limiting himself to what he regards as the facts or practical laws. The idealist, as he believes, is inclined to ignore the hard facts and is tempted to think of his devotion to ideals as a sufficient condition for their realization. Yet the realist in outlawing ideals has his drawbacks. The facts asserted by the realist are limited in scope. Ideals are also facts. One need not accept the doctrine that only power and self-interest are realities. What men aspire to are also causative factors in human pursuits. And, what is more, the realist despite his scorn of ideals has his own preferences, his own ideals, these usually being the *status quo*, the established, whatever is manifestly successful.

Yet one may accept a certain aspect of the realistic temper. One may learn from it to give greater importance to practical means in the pursuit of ideals. The idealist is in danger of regarding his ideal values as existing apart from reality; but as John Dewey argues with the idealist in mind, there is "the tragic need for the most realistic study of forces and consequences, a study conducted in a more scientifically accurate and complete manner than that of the professed *Real-politik*."[1] The idealist need not be a visionary person, nor need the realist be devoid of worthwhile ends.

Coming to the disillusioned, they remind us of the hopeless endeavors and even absurdities of human existence. They see bright expectations vanish one by one, each life facing final defeat. The list of thoughtful pessimists is long—Schopenhauer, Leopardi, Hardy, Anatole France, Chekhov, and in our time the existentialists and many others. They all make us aware of the darker aspects of life that make for anguish and ultimate despair.

The darker aspects of human existence have been variously described. For the Greek tragedians Aeschylus, Sophocles, and Euripides the deeply disturbing facts of life were the decrees of fate. Oedipus was not responsible for his tragic fate, since he was foredoomed to kill his father and marry his mother. The fate of Creon was similarly determined, his patriotic action eventually leading to the death of his wife and son. For Schopenhauer the hopes of life vanish one by one, and "life like a pendulum swings on, between desire unsatisfied which is pain, and desire satisfied which is ennui." For Thomas Hardy the world plays with its victims, stirs them with hopes and aspirations, and then after torturing them destroys them. For Anatole France the earth will gradually be uninhabitable and men will be shorn of their glory.

---

[1] *Reconstruction in Philosophy*, New York, Henry Holt & Co., 1920, p. 130.

"Some day the last of them will without hate and without love breathe the last sigh into the hostile heaven. And the earth will continue to revolve bearing through the silent spaces the ashes of humanity."[2] For the existentialists, as for instance Martin Heidegger and Jean-Paul Sartre, human life is an absurdity, being without rhyme or reason. One's life is the history of anxiety, dread, agony, and consciousness of guilt. Man is thrown into the world without his consent to do as best he can and then die.

From the pessimists we have much to learn; their careful reflections on life, their patient examination of despair, their deep understanding of human dilemmas, and their courageous rejection of easy solutions. They are certainly right in their protests against complacent optimism. As E. Singer says, "No longer is the portrayal in art of the gray and the dark, however unrelieved, taken for morbidity; nor should it ever have been, for nothing can be more wholesome than the discouragement of complacent optimism, nothing more salutary than this plain lesson—that hope in life, if it is to be had, is not to be had cheap."[3] Yet pessimists in their interpretations ignore certain aspects of human experience. Granting the truth of most of their descriptions one may yet accept the human situation with courage and strength. One should realize that life has its intrinsic value, that it has significance when functioning within its limited career, and that human beings have a share in molding the facts.

II

There is an alternative to the views as so far referred to. We live in a world where there are both good and evil, love and hatred, kindness and violence, magnificence and sordidness, wealth and poverty, success and failure, possibilities and rigid inevitabilities. In such a world, what William James calls meliorism is a more convincing attitude. Being neither pessimism nor optimism it is characterized by a sense of progress which does not underrate the existence of evil, accepting all the evidence for the darker aspects of life while at the same time acknowledging

---

2 *Le Jardin d' Épicure,* Paris, Calmann-Lévy, Éditeurs, pp. 26-27.

3 *On the Contented Life,* New York, Henry Holt & Co., 1923, p. 170.

the brighter aspects. It does not look for cosmic support of the triumph of good, yet it does believe that to a degree desirable possibilities are attainable through human intelligence, courage, and action. It is fully aware that the tragic element cannot be completely eliminated and that there is no certain guarantee for success and that human endeavors can be attended by failure, but it is quite willing to take the risks.

Meliorism implies certain commitments. First, for the meliorist the universe is pluralistic. This point was especially emphasized by William James. "The world we live in," he says, "exists diffused and distributed, in the form of an indefinitely numerous lot of *eaches,* coherent in all sorts of ways and degrees."[4] Secondly, the meliorist insists on freedom of choice. From the melioristic point of view human beings are not the puppets of fate, but face genuine alternatives and their decision is a factor in the shape of things. Finally, for the meliorist there are real possibilities. Every realized ideal is the expression of such a possibility. Ideals "are *live* possibilities, for we are their live champions and pledges, and if the complimentary conditions come and add themselves, our ideals will become actual things."[5]

What, then, is the nature of human fulfillment, and what are the conditions for it?

Before suggesting an answer to these questions, a few things must be said about the nature of man. Man is no longer considered as having been created by a god. He is a product of natural evolutionary processes. As a living being, his purpose is the common one of all living beings—self-preservation and type-preservation. But man as a "higher" form of living being has certain distinctive traits. His mental development has given him the power to control events by being able to predict consequences and he is therefore possessed of the anticipation and the resourcefulness necessary to the pursuit of desired ends. And the great modifiability of his biological drives has increased his desires and his determination to realize them. Finally, through cooperation, he has succeeded in developing civilization. Our concern is with

---

[4] *Pragmatism,* New York, Longman, Green & Co., 1913, p. 264.
[5] *Ibid.,* p. 287.

this type of being and with the nature of his fulfillment.

Man is primarily engaged in realizing his desires and these are normally involved in activities that are usually outward looking. In mating, in transacting business, in regulating political, economic, and social activities, and in pursuing knowledge, certain desires are involved that seek fulfillment. But one must judge the content of each desire and the consequences intelligently. The demands of desire must be guided by reason; the desirable rather than what is immediately desired should be pursued. It is possible to sacrifice what one really wants for something slight and ephemeral. A temporary indulgence in some pleasure is not necessarily wrong, but it may be wrong if it hindered the achievement of a permanent kind of satisfaction. The motive of action is seldom immediate pleasure, although pleasure remains the test of whether one is moving in the right direction.

The satisfactory mode of life has several levels. First, the good, or end pursued, must be more or less attainable. There are certain general urgent needs and demands that should be satisfied. Health, ambition, and love are such needs; their standards are more or less essentially the same even though these vary in different societies. These desires may acquire new meanings, but such possibilities are open to all. And as far as possible these attainable desires should be in harmonious relation and not merely a sum of desires. The normal self functions as a unitary whole, and its satisfaction must constitute a unitary state of feeling. Secondly, for a satisfactory mode of life there has to be something more than the pursuit of attainable ends—there must also be the pursuit of unattainable ends, ideals that are only approachable. What makes life worthwhile is not only immediate satisfactions, however necessary these may be, or a static state of adjustment, but continually progress towards supreme possibilities. As Dewey says, "The end is no longer a terminus or limit to be reached, . . . not perfection as a final goal, but the ever-enduring process of perfecting, maturing, refining is the aim of living."[6] Or as Singer succinctly says, ". . . contentment may lie for us in that most improbable of pursuits, the pursuit of the unattainable, the in-

---

6 *Reconstruction in Philosophy*, New York, Henry Holt & Co., 1920, p. 140.

finitely remote, the 'ideal.' "[7] It must be born in mind that ideals pursued are not unalterable, fixed goals, but rather goals that are modified and enriched in time by new meanings and realizations. This pursuit must of course be guided by an intelligent sense of reality. Nothing can be gained by pursuing ideals that are not relevant to the kind of the world we live in.

Though for a satisfactory life both the pursuit of attainable and unattainable ends is necessary, the present discussion will be concerned with the latter pursuit. What, then, are the common, universal ideals that are to be pursued? This issue will be analyzed in some detail later, but it may here be mentioned that they are the ideals of science, morality, and art. We need science, both pure and technological, to increase knowledge and the power that comes from knowledge; we need morality to bring about the kind of society in which individuals can flourish without destroying one another; we need art to renew the human spirit for greater human effort. The pursuit of these specific ideals when taken together may be said to constitute one's religion.

It will be argued that the necessary condition for the fulfillment of human life lies in the pursuit of ideals, and especially of the ideals that have been mentioned. But before examining these ideals something should be said in greater detail on the nature of man.

---

[7] *On the Contented Life*, New York, Henry Holt & Co., 1923, p. 140.

Chapter II

THE NATURE OF MAN

There are various images of man. He is considered to be godlike in his nature, or just a little below the angels, yet at times demonic in his notions. For Plato he is a creature who stands halfway between divinity and mortality. Aristotle regards him as a rational animal. For Hobbes his life is "solitary, poor, nasty, brutish and short." Condorcet, with a more generous outlook, describes him as a creature of infinite perfectibility. Marx gave him contrasting traits: the bourgeois is selfish, ruthless, possessive; the proletariat is equalitarian, cooperative, fraternal. For Freud he is driven by unconscious forces, by libido wishes, is restless, frustrated. One can continue presenting an indefinite number of other images as provided by theologians, philosophers, psychologists, or poets.

Amid such a confusing variety of characterizations of man, the safest guide to attain a reasonable understanding of him will be the empirical approach. For an empiricist, questions of fact must be answerable by experience. Yet the word "experience" is a weasel word with many different meanings. Sometimes it suggests immediacy of sensations and at other times inaccessible privacies; it can even suggest inarticulate mysticism. It is true that whatever we know is based on experience, but we must add the further assertion that a question of fact must be open to public verification. For the modern empiricist or the experimentalist a fact is communicable, publicly demonstrable.

The present analysis will be guided by still another basic principle, namely, that nature is the whole of reality. Nature includes everything that we know and everything that we might know—the stars, the moon, the earth, plants, animals, human beings, their achievements, their dreams, and their aspirations. More precisely stated, nature is what empirical science finds it to be and what completed science would find it to be. Thus, the nature of man should be examined as a natural phenomenon among other natural phenomena. Man is a product of nature, he emerges from it and goes back to it. His origin, growth, and eventual dissolution are in the physical, biological, and social setting.

I

From the empirical point of view, man must be described in terms of behavior, since only behavior is open to common observation. Yet in a behavioristic account of man one must avoid two extreme interpretations—the mechanistic and the dualistic.

The mechanist attempts to reduce psychological concepts to physical terms. R. Carnap, for instance, maintains that "All psychological statements can be translated into physical language. . . . In other words the definition of any psychological term reduces it to physical terms."[1] But although behavior is physical at every point, from the organization of the physical entities nonphysical qualities may emerge which are as genuine aspects of nature as the physical. To speak of thinking, wishing, and hoping in purely physical terms does not convey the actual meaning of these activities. The other extreme view to be avoided is that of the dualist. The dualist postulates over and above behavior an agent that is radically different from body. According to H. Bergson, "spirit can rest upon matter and consequently unite with it in the act of pure perception, yet nevertheless be radically distinct from it."[2] The dualist's emphasis on the teleological aspect of man's mental behavior is of some value, but the spiritual agent he introduces is not verifiable and therefore not acceptable to the empiricist.

What is empirically given is body and its behavior. There is no disembodied mind or spirit. Man is part of the physical world, and as such can be classified as a physical object; yet his behavior reveals properties such as adaptation, intelligence, and learning,

---

[1] *The Unity of Science*, trans. by M. Black, London, Kegan Paul, Trench, Trubner Co., 1954, pp. 71-72.

[2] *Matter and Memory*, trans. by N. M. Black and W. S. Palmer, New York, Macmillan, 1913, p. 294.

all of which should be classified as teleological processes. If in the grouping of physical elements new properties emerge, then these properties can be classified as their nature demands. The logician, especially the modern logician, is conversant with the fact that the same object may be put into different classes, depending on the property that is being focused upon. A dagger may be a useful weapon as well as a beautiful object; a book may be small in size as well as big in meaning; a man may be moral as a member of his family and yet immoral as a member of a political party.

Mechanism and teleology are different ways of interpreting natural events; they represent different classes of events which depend on different purposes. Some physical objects have, thus, a double description, both mechanical and teleological. Whether we classify objects on the basis of mechanism or teleology depends upon which aspect we wish to emphasize. Both are legitimate, neither type of explanation has priority or greater importance.

What, then, is the nature of the teleological explanation in terms of which a human being is to be explained?

In the teleological explanation, the question "Why?" about a particular object or event is answered by specifying its function or the goal towards which it moves. If I am asked what a watch is for, I can say "to indicate time." If I am asked why an amoeba moves, I can say "to get food." If I am asked why a doctor visits his patient, I can say "to examine him." In every instance of teleological activity there is a bias, a tendency towards a certain type of result. The purpose of an event is a biased result which that class of events is expected to accomplish. The expected result does not follow always, but only, as Aristotle would say, "for the most part." There are, of course, different levels of purpose. In some cases, the expectation is from the point of view of the observer who has had prior experience with the class of events in question, and not necessarily from the point of view of the purposive agent. On the highest level of purpose, such as intentional purpose, the agent himself may anticipate the result towards which he is actively moving.

In the medium of mechanism man is to be defined in terms of purposive behavior. His purpose as a living being is self-maintenance. All living beings, from the amoeba to man, are classified together not because of their common mechanical structure, in which respect they may all differ, but because of their common purpose. This purpose is verifiable through objective observation. We may take self-maintenance as the minimal purpose of living beings, but any self-maintaining being may also belong to other teleological classes, as for example, that of type-maintenance. This description provides a general picture of man as a living being, but as a higher form of life he exhibits certain distinctive types of behavior which enhance his resourcefulness in the pursuit of his ends as well as raise the level and dimension of his ends.

The distinctive purposive human traits that will be discussed here may be found to a degree on a "lower" level of life; but their full fruition exists only on the human level. These traits, moreover, are not isolated separate aspects of human behavior, but are vitally interrelated. Man in his normal behavior responds as a whole organism, as a self.

It should also be made clear that the present discussion is concerned with man when considered collectively rather than distributively. Distributively some men are intelligent and some are dull, some are emotionally healthy and some are sick. Collectively there exists the norm, which by some is embodied more adequately than by others.

II

The first distinctive characteristic of man is what might be called symbolic response. Symbolic response, in its widest sense, is response to the meanings of stimuli. It is not response to the immediacy of the stimulus, but to what the stimulus stands for, to what it represents as possible consequence or consequences. One who is buying a car does not see the cars merely in their qualitative immediacy, that is, as patches of blue, brown or green and as varied shapes, but as vehicles to drive. Or, again, a chess player does not respond to the objects on a chess board as mere objects, but as pawns or knights or bishops with certain consequences in the moves. Or a mathematician in his manipulation of mathematical figures does not respond to them solely in their immediacy, but as symbols related to one another in a certain way. In functional terms the distinctive trait of man in facing problems is his control of behavior by anticipation.

Symbolic response, which gives a new dimension to man, is futuristic in the sense that the future consequences of stimuli function as present stimuli, controlling behavior. In this respect, symbolic or anticipatory response is fundamentally different from reflex action. In reflex action there is a certain automatic pattern —a specific stimulus causes a specific response irrespective of environmental or organic conditions. Accidental swallowing starts a series of actions that follow each other in a set way. Anticipatory action, unlike automatic action, is prospective, the response is not merely to what is immediately given but also to what is expected. And anticipatory response is also different from instinctive response. In instinctive response there is a more or less innately determined pattern of action without distinct awareness of future consequences; in symbolic or anticipatory response the expected future consequences are significant. One who faces a coming storm does not respond merely to the darkness of clouds or to the chilling of the environment, but to the expected lightning and rain.

Symbolic response is also essentially experimental. This becomes obvious when the symbolic situation is uncertain or perplexing. When I see a person and am not certain whether he is an acquaintance of mine or a stranger I am involved in two incompatible responses: Should I greet him or pass him by? My responses are neither fixed reflex actions nor aimless movements, they are experimental, self-directed to settle the ambiguities of my judgment. Such an experimental action, though strikingly exemplified in uncertainty, pertains to some degree to all symbolic situations. In writing a letter, for example, though we know in general what we are going to write, the sentences take definite form as we proceed. We struggle with certain words if they have different meanings depending on the context. This experimental quality is equally true in our most casual symbolic situations. The object we notice may either require our further attention or may be regarded as irrelevant to our immediate situation. All symbolic response is a kind of experiment, a reconstruction of the present behavior with reference to future results. Symbolic response in all of its forms is not mechanical or photographic action, but teleological and experimental.

There are levels of symbolic response. On one level the response is to the meaning of a perceived object. One responds to a blade as something that is sharp, to a chair as a comfortable seat. Animals to a degree have this type of response. The dog observing a chair jumps and rests itself upon it; the beast in observing its prey is in readiness to pounce upon it. On another level symbolic response is a natural sign-response. A natural sign indicates the existence of another event that has occurred or will occur. Rising smoke signifies fire, gathering clouds portend that it will rain, the ringing door bell suggests that the postman has arrived. Animals respond to natural signs. Pavlov's dogs were conditioned to the ringing bell as a sign of coming food; domesticated animals respond to a whip or to the master's voice. On a higher level, the distinctively human one, symbols do not merely signify, as natural signs do, another past or future event, like smoke signifying fire, but they convey the conception of events, and conceptions are not the events themselves but their meaning. In thinking or "talking *about* things we have conceptions of them, not the things themselves; and *it is the conceptions, and not the things, that symbols directly 'mean.' "*[3] It is language that functions in this latter sense of symbols. One responds to the word "fire" as a symbol that conveys the concept of burning, and to the word "bread" as a symbol that conveys the concept of edibility. This type of human response separates man from animals. And as E. Cassirer says, in reference to symbols in this latter sense, "The principle of symbolism, with its universality, validity, and general applicability, is the magic word, the Open Sesame! giving access to the specifically human world, to the world of human culture. Once man is in possession of this magic key further progress is assured."[4]

---

[3] Langer, Susanna K., *Philosophy in a New Key,* New York, Pelican Books Edition, 1948, p. 49.

[4] *An Essay on Man,* New York, Doubleday Anchor Books, 1953, p. 55.

Language in all its forms is perhaps the greatest invention of man. Through language, abstractions and generalization are attained, and so science, morality, art, and religion are developed. Through language, human beings are able to communicate and to partici- pate in common activities and to create culture and civilization.

What are the bearings of symbolic response on man's be- havior? Functionally symbolic response is behavior controlled by anticipation—it is intelligence. From the origin of man to the present day, he has shown amazing resourcefulness in the pursuit of goals. Primitive man's ingenuity to get food and shelter and his descendants' creation of language and their numerous inven- tions and technological developments are definite expressions of human versatility or intelligence. Man has gone far beyond other living beings in his efficient use of means for ends. Intelligence is based on symbolic response, on the power to foresee the results of coming events and to act in the light of these results. A re- sourceful or intelligent person is aware of the possibilities of success in his present activities.

Symbolic response is also the basis of human ideals. Human beings through their use of symbolic activity project desirable, ideal possibilities. Man finds his full stature in the pursuit of these possibilities, of meanings which transcend his immediate needs and conditions. These ideals are the most constructive forces in human life, bringing glory and new power to human existence. Yet there are some human possibilities that may result in violence and destruction far beyond the ferocities of the lower animal world.

III

There is a second distinctive characteristic of man—plasticity of drives. Organic life is primarily an urge or a drive. Human beings have all the basic needs of animals—food, sexual satisfac- tion, shelter—yet through learning and cultural development, made possible by symbolic response, they can develop new ends, values and ideals. The world of human values is rich and multi- farious. This phase of man must now be turned to.

His behavior differs from that of "lower" living beings in

that he is not so rigidly organized by innate propensities. The flight of birds, the mating of mammals, and the killing activity of beasts of prey are basically instinctive in the sense of inherited dispositions. That man's activities are rooted in basic needs and drives is to be accepted, but their changeless rigidity is doubtful. Some years ago, psychologists like William McDougall overemphasized the instinctive aspect of human nature. After arguing that instinctive impulses determine the ends of all human activities, he resolved man's activities into a definite number of instincts —parenthood, pugnacity, acquisition, constructiveness, gregariousness, and many others. Against this fixed notion of human instincts other psychologists, like John Watson, carried the fluidity of drives to extremes.

The truth seems to lie between these two extreme views. There are basic human drives, inner propensities, yet these have within them considerable plasticity. Drives are pivots for the further organization and development of human activities. A basic response like fear is not a fixed instinct; in different situations there are different forms of fear, the fear of financial failure, for instance, being different from the fear of failure in love. Physiologically fears may have some common factor, yet qualitatively they differ. Similarly, such deep-rooted drives as the need of food and sexual activity have many different forms. One's need of food may be regulated as to quantity and quality and manner of consumption. Sex drives may be purely biological or highly psychological, romantic or pathological.

The modification of human drives has two poles—the biological and the social. There are the basic or biological drives and yet there are the social forces, like tradition, customs, institutions, and the educational processes, that mold human nature. Human nature is thus in the making, never a finished product. One is born into a family and from the first day is being molded by his elders. A survey of human history shows striking modifications in the human being. As Lewis Mumford points out, there is the archaic man, earthbound, limited to planting, the mating of animals, and his marriage; there is the early civilized man, ruled

5 *Outline of Psychology*, New York, Scribner, 1923, Chapter V.

by kings and enslaved by the system; there is the axial man, devoted to transcendental ideals; there is the old-world man, developing art and industry; there is the new-world man, obsessed with money and technology; and there may be the future man, pursuing new ideals.[6]

In the early stage of the individual the basic or biological drives may be limited to a few primitive ones like hunger, thirst, and sexual desire. And these drives may be what B. F. Skinner regards as "a convenient way of referring to the effects of deprivation and satiation."[7] Yet these drives gradually develop into relatively independent motives and interests. Empirically it is a fact that on the human level various interests emerge and that the motives of them are not mere deprivation and satiation as of the primitive desires. Some contemporary psychologists tend to reduce human motives to a limited number of primitive drives. Such a theory is the result of the "genetic fallacy." Just because hunger, thirst, and the sexual desire are the original drives in the individual's life, it does not follow that in his further growth no new motives develop. In later life new motives arise, and the variety of these motives gives to human action a greater degree of freedom and significance.

Drives in their developed forms become interests, and as interests they are biased anticipatory responses. Interests are not mere impulses or mere anticipations, they are anticipatory responses that signify a disposition to bring about results. Ralph B. Perry says, "To expect an event signifies only a disposition to act *on* it; while to be interested in an event signifies a disposition to act *for* it, or to provide an occasion for acting on it."[8] If I merely anticipate that my friend will offer me a drink, my nervous system is in readiness to receive it, but if I wish my friend to offer me a drink, the readiness to receive it is in agreement with my wish to drink.

Interests take different forms. To begin with, they may be

---

[6] Mumford, Lewis, *The Transformation of Man*, New York, Har-Rowe, 1956, Chapters II-VI.

[7] *Science and Human Behavior*, New York, Macmillan, 1953, p. 144.

[8] *General Theory of Value*, New York, Longman, Green & Co., 1926, p. 318.

positive or negative. This polarity of interests has been expressed in different ways: appetite and aversion, pleasure and pain, abience and adience, good and evil. Positive interests demand the presence of a result, whereas negative interests demand its absence. Interests may also be general or specific. Hunger, for example, may be satisfied by anything that is edible, but it may also demand some specific food. Affection may be attached to a number of people, but it may also be attached to only one. Whereas Plato argued for the love of the universal, Royce liked to argue that love is not love unless it has made its object irreplaceable.

It should be noticed that man throughout his career is not only concerned with the fulfillment of his basic drives and interests but is vitally concerned with comparative and preferential desires. On a rather low ideational level, preference is habitual; there is no clear distinction between alternative consequences of the human being's choices. The great bulk of man's choices are on this level. On a higher level, preferences are made through rules. Rules are guides to preferences. Being formulas that cover typical situations, they enable one to meet such situations in advance. On a still higher ideational level, preferences are made through principles. Here one goes beyond rules. Instead of asking what one is to do, one asks why it should be done; in other words, what far-reaching results are expected from a given result. These preferential responses are concerned with human needs as qualified by chosen desires. The chosen ends are the ones that satisfy these needs or desires. The "better" is the desirable rather than only the desired, the "better" or "best" is meaningful only in relation to a conflict of desires, since apart from this conflict there is no meaning to choice. The function of reason is not to rival desire, but rather to survey the situation impartially; the objects desired and the desires themselves are examined to the end of determining how all the desires, if possible, may be satisfied or integrated.

Human beings, of course, do not always make wise choices. Man has basic primitive drives, so that some of his actions may be violent, irrational, aggressive, too self-regarding. Especially when caught in the violent hatreds of his group, man's rationality is a source of destruction. And, again, sometimes man falsifies facts to himself as well as to others and rationalizes his motives and confuses his behavior. Psychoanalytic studies have made these aspects of human behavior much clearer. Psychoanalysts have also emphasized the fact that some of our deeper affective drives have their roots in the unconscious and so are difficult to control. We must not ignore or evade these and similar recalcitrant aspects of human nature; they are reminders to us that the remaking of man is an endless task.

And yet the conception of the relative plasticity of human drives is a liberating one. It means that most of the evils of the world—destructive economic competition, suppressive sex taboos, racial hatreds, and, above all, wars—are not the results of unalterable instincts. These and similar evils are not inevitable. The rule of justice, of equality and cooperation, is a genuine possibility. Individuals are in the process of making themselves, and this could be in the direction of ideal ends. Take war as an example. For centuries human beings have been involved in frequent wars. In our supposedly civilized era we have passed through two world wars and are witnessing wars in Vietnam, in the Middle East, and in Africa. And yet the citizens of one country do not hate the citizens of another through instinct. It is true that such psychological tendencies as pugnacity, hatred, and ambition are channelled into war activity; yet war is primarily a social rather than a psychological phenomenon. Traditions, national customs, and economic institutions are the major causes of war and these causes are changeable aspects of human behavior, however stubborn, and not unchangeable instincts.

The issue whether human nature can change is of paramount individual and social importance. As John Dewey says, "The theory that human nature is unchangeable is . . . the most depressing and pessimistic of all possible doctrines. If it were carried out logically, it would mean a doctrine of predestination from birth that would outdo the most rigid of theological doctrines. . . . The existence of almost every conceivable kind of social institution at some time and place in the history of the world is evidence of the plasticity of human nature."[9]

IV

The third distinctive characteristic of man is consciousness. Consciousness is often considered the most important phase of human life. We speak of the inorganic world as devoid of life, and of most living beings as devoid of consciousness, of awareness, that is, of what they do or of what they will do. A man without consciousness would hardly be considered a human being. To lose our consciousness would be to lose our identity, our unique selfhood. What then is consciousness? What does it mean to be conscious of something?

The concept of consciousness has given a great deal of difficulty to psychologists and philosophers. There is a great deal of ambiguity about its meaning. For some psychologists the study of man is the study of his consciousness, while for others this is a fruitless concept and therefore should be discarded. There is one widely used meaning of consciousness, the one with its roots in the classic empiricism of Locke and Hume, that ought to be discarded, namely, consciousness as the immediacy of experience. From this point of view each person has a private, unsharable world which belongs to him and is inaccessible to others. For the modern empiricist with his belief that all questions of fact are open to the experimental approach, the word "consciousness" has the meaning it had prior to the classic empiricist's interpretation. *Con* added to *scious* refers to participation in another's experience rather than private unsharable immediacy. This sharing phase of mind takes two forms—self-consciousness and other-consciousness.

First as to self-consciousness. Having an experience like the sensation of green or like the feeling of anger and being conscious of the experience are two distinct things. The concept of unconscious experience is not meaningless. Frequently we see, we hear, we touch, we feel, we select or reject without being conscious of our experience. The transition to self-consciousness or introspec-

---

[9] *Problems of Men*, New York, Greenwood Press, Publishers, 1968, p. 191.

tion is a simple one. In introspection the response is to an earlier experience, be it a sensation, a perception, an emotion, or a belief. We introspect a perception of a landscape by responding to our earlier perception of the landscape, and we introspect a feeling of anger by responding to our earlier experience of anger. There is no introspective consciousness without memory. Thus to have consciousness there must be at least two mental events, an original one and a later one. In more behavioristic terms, introspective consciousness is had whenever an individual cognitively responds to his prior response as stimulus. Conscious response is reflexive anticipatory response.

It should also be noted that one's introspective claim must be checked and that this checking must be done outside the limits of introspection, for immediate availability does not mean unquestionable verification.

Consciousness is also other-consciousness. The mind knows not only its own experience but also the experience of others. Everyday langauge indicates this possibility when one says, "I am conscious of my neighbor's predicament," or "Friends are conscious of each other's secrets."

The common-sense view which takes the existence of other minds for granted deserves more respect. It should be noted, to begin with, that the contents of the other mind—perceptions or ideas—are not exclusively private. The landscape that the other mind perceives or the mathematical equation of which it thinks can also be the contents of my mind. The notion that one's mental contents are exclusively one's own is based on what R. B. Perry calls the "fallacy of exclusive particularity." It is true that another's perceptions and ideas are his own and that they cannot be separated from his mind, but these facts do not imply that his mental contents may not also be my mental contents. The same principle applies to my knowledge of the pain or sensation of the other mind. To know another's pain or sensation I need not have his pain or sensation. Another's somatic and proprioceptive senses belong to his nervous system; yet I can determine the degree of his pain by noticing the amount of anodyne he takes and I can experimentally determine the intensity and the quality of his sensation.

The bearing of consciousness on human behavior is far-reaching. First as to self-consciousness. It is through self-consciousness, as this has been described, that one attains unity of self. Unity of self is not due to a soul or psyche residing in the body; structurally the unity is the biological organism, behaviorally it is the integrated self through consciousness. As it takes two minds to make a mind—my earlier and my present one—in consciousness these two are unified.

Secondly as to other-consciousness. In other-consciousness genuine communication emerges. Communication must have a common reference. If two people understand each other there must be something in common between the two minds. And what is in common is the meaning that is exhibited in behavior. The common meaning is not some private psychic entity in the inaccessible minds of individuals who communicate with each other, but is due to observable behavior. With this communication we have the possibility of transmitting acquired characteristics and hence of developing culture.

V

The final distinctive characteristic of man is being a self or personality. Though the traditional idea of soul has been discarded by many, a naturalistic notion of self assimilates and enlarges its significance and function. In man, the characteristics so far considered—symbolic response, plasticity of drives, and consciousness—are relatively unified to form a functional structure. Although the term 'self' or 'personality' is sometimes used to refer to individual peculiarities, to the way one talks, walks, or laughs, it sometimes denotes a mode of structural unity in the individual.

That which characterizes a self in the more serious sense consists of the way one's behavior is organized or unified. Through the pervasive factor of the symbolic response or cognition, the self is time-binding, space-binding, and goal-binding.

The self is time-binding, for it remembers the past and antici-
pates the future; it is space-binding, for it relates the distant to
the near; it is goal-binding, for it takes account of different
demands and determines which is central and which is vital.
One's true self is one's unified deepest desires and uppermost
aspirations in the temporal and spatial setting.

This empirical approach to the conception of a soul or self
has been made by psychologists. For G. W. Allport "personality
is the dynamic organization within the individual of those psy-
chophysical systems that determine his characteristic behavior and
thought."[10] Similarly for H. A. Murray the self or personality is
the unity of action: "Man is a 'time-binding' organism, which is
a way of saying that, by conserving some of the past and antici-
pating some of the future, a human being can, to a significant
degree, make his behavior accord with events that have happened
as well as those that are to come. Man is not a mere creature of
the moment, at the beck and call of any stimulus or drive."[11]

The self is a behavioral, functional unity but not a unit.
One need not hypostatize the notion of the self. Holistic descriptions court the danger of oversimplification. In describing the
self as a functional unity one should not ignore its constituent
parts, its complexity, its variations in different environmental
settings. Finally, it should also be noted that the self is an unfinished unity—the self is in the making. The environmental
conditions and the daily decisions mold and shape the self. Man
can use his powers for destruction and self-destruction; he can
also use them for the fulfillment of beneficial ideals.

---

10 *Pattern and Growth in Personality*, New York, H R & W, 1961, p. 28.
11 *Explorations in Personality*, New York, Oxford U Pr 1939, p. 49.

Chapter III

IDEALS

Human beings are purposive in their activities. Some of these activities are irrational and chaotic, while others are rational and orderly, and some are self-centered and egoistic, while others are generous and altruistic. Some activities are frustrated and never develop into their possibilities, while others find full expression and result in unexpected achievements. The purposive activities of human beings are not wholly fixed; they exhibit certain tendencies but these tendencies are modifiable and offer wide possibilities. Some contemporary psychologists even question the existence of instincts in human beings. Human beings have certain basic needs and drives, yet most of their activities, it is claimed, are the results of conditioning and the formation of habits. Eating habits may vary from immediate satisfaction of hunger to leisurely, civilized dining; the sex impulse may be limited to biological fulfillment or go beyond it to romantic expression; aggression may move from the desire to have power over other human beings to the desire to have power to remove human inequalities.

The normal, healthy activities of human beings are usually outward looking. There are mystics for whom inner contemplation is supreme, and there are hedonists for whom pleasure is the final value, but for most human beings objective consequences are important. Satisfaction for the latter is the reward for the successful fulfillment of objectives. The most we can say about life is that it is concerned with activities that are interesting, satisfying, and to a degree important.

Human activities may be classified into two major types. First, there are those in which the pursuit is of immediate, attainable objectives—the daily tasks, professional duties, passing delights, finite loves. Secondly, there are those in which the pursuit is of enduring, weighty ideals—knowledge, power, wealth, abundance, art, equality, justice. These two types of activities should not be too sharply distinguished, yet they are sufficiently different to be examined separately. The major concern here will be with the second type of human pursuits, with those in quest of ideals.

I

Ideals have a varied function in life. For some they are the most dynamic, worthwhile goals in life, while for others they are mere fantasies that provide escape from the harsh facts of life. And for some they are the sustaining forces in their daily routine work, while for others they are the strong incentives in their restless ambitious pursuits. Ideals are also vital forces in the life of societies. For some groups they promote beneficial social enterprise, while for other groups they promote the intensification of tyrannical power over others. Thus there are destructive ideals as well as those that are beneficial. Before examining the nature of ideals one must state one's basic philosophic perspective in relation to them. Three important historic perspectives will be considered: the theistic, the idealistic, and the naturalistic.

For theism belief in a personal, transcendent God is central. The dominant monotheistic religions—Judaism, Christianity, Mohammedanism—proclaim a god as the creator of the universe and the source of ultimate power. Beyond the natural world there is the supernatural world and the destiny of the natural world depends on a Power beyond itself. Yet there are differences among the theists. Most theists are absolutists—God is all-knowing, all-powerful, all-good. For the absolute theists the object of worship is infinite in power and ideally perfect. But some theists, to account for the disturbing facts of suffering, injustice, and evil, resort to the idea of a finite god. In the religion of the Parsees the good principle, Ahura Mazda, is in conflict with the evil principle, Angra Mainyu. Here the divine power is limited and it is man's duty to fight for the good. Similarly for many modern theists the divine being is essentially good but limited in power.

But a limited god is obviously not ideal as an object of worship. What, then, is the status of ideals in theism?

The theist finds the source of ideals in the will of God. In this interpretation, ideals like justice, righteousness, and the universal brotherhood of man are not merely human aspirations, but revelations of the will of God. This view found expression in the declaration of the Hebrew prophets, in the thoughts of the Apostle Paul and of St. Augustine, and also of the medieval theologians and Martin Luther. A similar view is to be found in many contemporary theologians.

The theistic interpretation of ideals has its negative and positive aspects. Negatively ideals apart from God are considered of little significance if not misleading. Man as a depraved creature is unable to discover the true ideals, he is finite and limited and thus his ideals are purely relative. Man has the temptation to exalt his ideals as if he himself were a god. For theists the very source of sin is "man's willful refusal to acknowledge the finite and determinate character of his existence."[1] According to them, human reason cannot give us the ideals by which human life should be guided.

Positively ideals are to be received from God. For theologians like Karl Barth ideal values are completely dependent upon the sovereign and free revelation of God — that is to say upon the supernatural word of God. Karl Barth declares, "God's revelation is a ground which has no sort of higher or deeper ground above or behind it, but is simply a ground in itself, and therefore as regards man an authority from which no appeal to a higher authority is possible."[2] Yet we can never fully grasp this revelation. The word of God is not granted to mankind, it is given to "this and that particular man." For E. H. Brunner the good depends on the Will of God, what God wills is good, what opposes his will is evil. "The good is that which God does; the goodness of man can be no other than letting himself be placed

---

[1] Niebuhr, R., *The Nature and Destiny of Man*, New York, Scribner, 1943, Vol. 1, p. 177.

[2] *The Doctrine of the Word of God*, trans, by G. T. Thompson, New York, Scribner, 1955, p. 350.

within the activity of God." [3] In a similar though more qualified spirit R. Niebuhr maintains that in the personal life "the
moral experience consists of the sense of moral obligation as
being laid upon man not by himself, nor yet by his society but
by God."[4] Similarly, Jacques Maritain when writing about the
ideal values of morality has this to say: ". . . only the transcendent
God who is Subsistent Truth can in the last analysis establish
a moral law and moral values which impose themselves on the
conscience in an unconditional way — and without which there
is no longer anything to guide our conduct." [5]

The theistic interpretation of ideals despite its effort to gain
a perspective beyond human limitations faces many difficulties.
If man's thoughts are so corrupt, as the theologians assert, it is
difficult to conceive how they can function fruitfully in human
experience. It is true that man is finite, limited in knowledge
and often confused in his judgment, yet his intelligence is one
of the most valuable guides in his life. It is worth noting that
if human thought is so impotent to form valid ideas, logically
the theistic theories would have no tenable basis. And revelation,
the favorite source of enlightenment for the theist, is not available to most of us, especially to the empirical philosophers. Thus
the function of ideals becomes too heavily dependent on theological commitments which are at best dubious. The pursuit of
ideals need not depend on theistic beliefs. Many ideals are significant apart from theistic beliefs. The ideals of justice, equality,
and universal good don't need any supernatural support for
their value, being meaningful in human relations whether there
be a god or not. In fact, the ideal values attributed to God are
idealizations of human values.

Another important historic perspective is idealism. In the
East idealism originated in India, and in the West in Greece. It
has a long and distinguished career. Idealism has so many variations that to formulate a description that will apply to all of

---

[3] *The Divine Imperative*, trans. by Olive Wyon, Philadelphia, The Westminster
Press, 1936, p. 55.

[4] *The Nature and Destiny of Man*, New York, Scribner, 1943, Vol. I, p. 137.

[5] *Moral Philosophy*, New York, Scribner, 1944, p. 444.

them is not possible. Yet idealism as such has certain basic ideas. Idealism is a philosophy of hope and aspiration; thus it interprets reality in terms of the highest human categories, like Mind and Spirit. For most idealists reality is Mind or Spirit. For Berkeley *esse est percipi;* for Hegel the real is rational and the rational is real; for Schopenhauer reality is a Universal Will. Such idealists are definitely mentalists or spiritualists. And yet there has been another important trend in idealism — the Platonic. Plato was not a mentalist, for him the final real things are Ideas, and Ideas are not mental images but objective forms, essences, prototypes. Of these the most important ones are the Ideas of truth, goodness, and beauty, and the supreme idea is the good. There is one other distinction to be made in idealism. Some, like Hegel, are monists for whom reality is a unified rational system, the Whole, the Absolute; and others, like Leibnitz, are pluralists for whom reality is a society of minds rather than one Universal Mind. The pluralists wish to retain the integrity of the individual.

What, then, is the bearing of idealism on ideals? Before answering this question one should distinguish metaphysical idealism from the practical, common-sense view of idealism. The metaphysical idealists are not necessarily the sole guardians of ideals. It is possible to have ideals on a different philosophical basis and even without any well-worked-out philosophic outlook. And yet many metaphysical idealists feel that in their systems they provide a firmer rooting for ideals.

First, these idealists believe that ideals have an independent ontological status, being in the very structure of the universe and not merely human aspirations. Human reason or feeling may discern ideals, but neither creates them. For Plato the ideals of truth, goodness, and beauty are independent realities. Particular judgments of truth, particular actions of the good, particular objects of beauty are dim revelations of corresponding ideas. In modern idealism, especially for Hegel and for Hegelians like Bradley and Bosanquet, ideals are aspects of the Absolute. The real is ideal and the ideal is real. For N. Hartmann, a recent important idealist, ideals are disclosed in value-feeling, yet have an "ideal existence." Indeed, there is a realm of values which subsists in itself. As Hartmann says, "Values have self-existence. Values subsist independently of the consciousness of them. Consciousness can grasp or miss them, but cannot make them." [6] And as is also maintained, ideals are not relative but absolute. They are not merely social, cultural, or historic phenomena, but constitute an absolute principle of perfection.

Finally, ideals are eternal, changeless perfections. This doctrine was especially dear to Plato. For Greek thought change was non-being, imperfection. The same view persists, though with some modification, in Absolute Idealism. For F. H. Bradley nothing that is real moves; for Bosanquet the ideal is what we can only see in the context of the whole. The drive of experience is "towards the whole to which it belongs, and every self to its completion in the Absolute, and of which the Absolute itself is at once an incarnation and a satisfaction." [7] Or the spirit of totality "is the clue to reality, value and freedom." [8]

Idealistic theories of ideals have a long history and have widely permeated human thought; but an empiricist finds it difficult to accept most of the claims. Ideals have reality, but this reality is not independent of human beings. The realities of ideals are the aspirations of human beings. We know nothing of ideals as an objective structure of the universe. Ideals have no meaning apart from human desires. Although ideals have transcendence, this lies solely in human aspiration for perfection. Although ideals have also a certain absoluteness, this is purely functional, pertaining to them only as moving forces. Actually they are born and grow in different settings, and many decay in time.

Naturalism, like idealism, has a long history and many variations. The description of naturalism will be limited to its contemporary development and primarily to its development in this country as expressed in the philosophies of Santayana, Dewey, Woodbridge, and many others. Three interrelated points will be

---

6 *Ethics*, New York, Macmillan, 1932, Vol. I, p. 218.

7 *The Principle of Individuality and Value*, London, Macmillan, 1912, p. 340

8 *Ibid.*, p. 23.

mentioned. First, for the naturalist the empirical method is the means of getting reliable knowledge, this being the method that employs the rationally verifiable procedure of science, this term to be used in a generous sense. This procedure must eliminate most of the claims of the intuitionists, rationalists, and revelationists. Secondly, for the naturalists the world of reality is the world of nature, from atoms to human beings and their aspirations, and inclusive of the astronomical world. This commitment rejects the supernatural world with all its traditional religious implications. Thirdly, for the naturalists, especially for the leading American representatives, all qualities of nature are regarded as real and not as mere appearances. Contemporary naturalism is not a reductive philosophy.

From the naturalistic point of view ideals have their roots within the temporal, natural setting of human experience. As Santayana eloquently says, "Everything ideal has a natural basis and everything natural an ideal development." [9] Ideals have no ontological status apart from human aspirations; they are possibilities within the natural world, generated by natural conditions and sustained by human efforts. Ideals of individual relations, of society, of science and of art are natural goals, being products of the human imagination, so that their meaning and value can only be obscured by extranatural involvements.

For naturalists ideals function within human activities, yet there are differences of emphasis. Some naturalists emphasize the biological aspect of ideals, others the psychological or the social, and still others the historical. All these descriptions of the function of ideals have their importance, and yet one need not limit one's interpretation to a single context. The view that seems most fruitful and that will be entertained in this discussion is that of contextual naturalism.

For the contextual naturalist ideals are natural aspirations that function in a variety of contexts. To understand the nature and the function of an ideal one must examine its specific context where alone it is meaningful or pragmatically fruitful. The ideal of love has meaning in the biological, psychological, and

---

[9] *The Life of Reason,* New York, Scribner, 1905-6, Vol. I., p. 21.

social setting. The ideal of equality has relevance in the human, cultural, and historic setting. To argue for the ideal of deathless existence would be to argue for an ideal that has no natural, human context. For superhuman beings immortality may be a relevant issue, but not for human beings, all of whom are mortal.

Because ideals have their origin and fruition within the natural world they should not therefore be demeaned. There is a long and unfortunate tradition that believes that to glorify and to esteem values one has to relate them to some supernatural or extranatural realm. There is no reason why the value of ideals should be anchored to religious beliefs or idealistic philosophies. If certain ideals have value they will be valuable in all philosophical perspectives. Since ideals are emergents of natural conditions, we have good reason to say, "How wonderful is the natural world!"

II

Ideals are many and varied. There are individual ideals as well as social ideals. The ideal of an artist is to create objects of beauty; the ideal of a scientist is to explore the secrets of nature; the ideal of a business man is to accumulate wealth. The Machiavelian ideal is to attain power at any cost. The ideal of a democratic society is the freedom, equality, and happiness of all men alike. Peace is a noble ideal. The ideals in all these illustrations are not immediate needs to be satisfied nor irresponsible imaginings to be indulged in; they are aspirations for more remote satisfactions. Ideals are worthy possibilities of some weight, endurance and meaning that stir men to greater achievement. Logically ideals are not propositions that may be either true or false. The ideal of universal brotherhood is not a statement of truth, but rather a statement that one wishes to be true. Nor are ideals like rules to be obeyed. Do not steal your neighbor's property is not an ideal but an order. Ideals are proposals to be achieved; they are proposals to be changed to propositions. The ideal realm is, as Dewey says, "that collection of imagined possibilities that stimulates men to new efforts and realizations." [10]

10 *Reconstruction in Philosophy*, New York, Henry Holt & Co., 1924, p. 118.

Some of the dominant characteristics of ideals are worth considering.[11]

First, ideals are desired or more desirable possibilities, that is, with worthwhile consequences. One whose ideal is to accumulate wealth, or to attain a position of power, or to get more and more knowledge looks forward to the possibilities that he wishes or aspires to. Similarly, the ideals of groups, whether the groups be small or large, express aspiration. The ideal of the Greeks was a high civilization, the ideal of the Romans was world domination, the ideal of the Medievalists was a theocratic society, the ideal of the founders of the American nation was democracy all of these, quite obviously, were regarded as desirable possibilities.

The notion of the desirable possibility needs more clarification. An immediate desire or a passing fancy does not characterize ideals. The desires that characterize ideals are more enduring and more critically evaluated; the aim is to be considered as having worthy consequences. Ideals always involve the notion of better or best in the sphere of values. One finds an ideal not only desirable but worthy of achievement.

The concept of possibility, one must realize, has an ambiguous meaning. It may mean potency in our natural world or just some imaginary possibility with no relevance to actuality. Ideals are concerned with existential possibilities, for their urge is to actually realize aspirations. Human beings aspired for more effective and speedier travel and communication and they more or less succeeded in attaining these desires through steamboats, trains, airplanes, telegrams, and telephones. All these were possibilities in the natural conditions. But the desire to enjoy the society and culture of mermaids and griffins, however appealing, is in the realm of the purely imaginary. Significant ideals are within the realm of actual possibilities.

Secondly, ideals are motives for dynamic action. The ideal of human rights or equality or a moral society is not a mere intellectual abstraction but a valid incentive to action. Not only moral ideals, but other types of ideals — political, religious, and

---

11 For an excellent discussion of this issue see Edel, A., *Method in Ethical Theory*, London, Routledge & Kegan Paul, 1963, Chapter XV.

aesthetic — are dynamic forces. Political ideals have always prompted action; religious ideals have not only demanded worship but action as well; aesthetic ideals have also been dynamic since the apprehension of beauty, as Plato maintains in the *Symposium,* involving the desire for birth into beauty.

Some have ignored the dynamic nature of ideals. For some, ideals have been primarily objects of contemplation and a haven from the conflicts of existence; for others they have been objects of worship, any contact with natural human needs being regarded as the lowering of the status of ideals; for still others, they have been mere illusions with no real relevance to the hard facts of life. These and similar negativistic views of ideals may have some justification in life, but the ideals that have real significance in life are those that stir us to action.

The dynamic nature of ideals is based on human needs and demands. Ideals are projections of human desires against the frustrations and limitations of life. The firmer and deeper the basis of the desires, the firmer and deeper the impulse toward action. Ideals that are imposed by authority or custom lack vitality; it is those that attract the individual or the group that have the truly dynamic nature.

Thirdly, ideals are the basis for the activities of individuals and groups. The ideal of democracy is the basis for the activities that constitute the democratic way of life; it is the guiding principle for the political, economic, educational, and other activities. The ideal of democracy provides the principle for the selection of the means for the desired end. As Dewey has emphasized, in all meaningful activities means and ends form a continuum. Ideals function as the organizing principle in the means-and-ends continuum.

Fourthly, ideals have a certain remoteness. They should not be identified with the daily attainable objectives. Most of the time our interests and activities do not reach beyond the next day. Everyday pressures constrain us and absorb our energies. Ideals look to the future, to what is to be, they are aspirations over a longer stretch of time. Ideals in time grow and are enriched in their meanings and possibilities, and by their very demands are approachable but never fully attainable. The attainment of the ideals of knowledge, of power, of a moral society, and of a world civilization might be said to require an infinite stretch of time. The pursuit of ideals is, to repeat, the pursuit of the unattainable, yet two different notions of the unattainable should be distinguished. The effort to fill a leaky cask with water is, in the strict sense, an unattainable task. But a mathematician working on a series of rational values may approach the irrational $\sqrt{2}$, though he may never reach the limiting conception. Progress towards ideals is akin to the mathematician's pursuit.

Finally, and most significantly, the pursuit of ideals is a source of contentment. As a recent American philosopher maintains, contentment lies "for us in that most improbable of pursuits, the pursuit of the unattainable, the infinitely remote, the 'ideal'." [12] For contentment the fulfillment of our everyday attainable objectives is necessary, but this is not sufficient; we need especially to be involved in pursuits that give us a sense of indefinite progress. Attainable objectives and unattainable ideals are interrelated, yet sharply distinguishable. King Solomon, who rejoiced in his pursuit of daily attainable objectives, ends with a melancholy reflection: "I looked on all my works that my hands had wrought, and all the labor that I had labored to do; and beheld that it was all vanity and vexation of spirit, and there was no profit under the sun." In contrast, William James gives a truer direction to life when he says, ". . . let the orientalists and pessimists say what they will, the thing of deepest — or, at any rate, of comparatively deepest — significance in life does seem to be its character of *progress*, or that strange union of reality with ideal novelty which it continues from one moment to another to present." [13]

III

The nature of ideals may further be clarified by indicating the relation of the ideal to the real. Human beings from the earliest period of their history have resorted to imagination, to

12 Singer, E. A., *On the Contented Life,* New York, Henry Holt & Co., 1923, p. 140.
13 *Talks to Teachers on Psychology,* etc., New York, Henry Holt & Co., 1912, p. 204.

the projection of their wishes in contrast with the harsh facts of life. Religion, poetry, and myths were developed prior to science, prose, and factual descriptions.

The contrast between the ideal and the real has resulted in the perennial dispute between the "idealists" and the "realists," using these terms in their general, practical sense. The realist has claimed that the real facts of the world are power, self-interest, and conflict of interests. Ideals are thought to be at best nothing more than sentiments with no vital relevance to economic, political, or international conflicts. But the realist's realism does not convey the full picture of life. What are the real facts of life? It is not true that the only real facts are power, self-interest, and conflicts; ideas, ideals, and cooperative activities are also determining factors in human affairs. The raw material of human nature is not fully fixed; the very idea of history involves variation, and on the human level ideals are factors that bring about desirable variations.

And, also, the realist often refers to success or dominance as the mark of the real. What is is right, what ought to be is illusory. But such a standard can hardly be a guide to life. Is success to be conceived as something of the moment or as achievable in the long run? There is a more fundamental objection to the realist's standard of success — it is unheroic in flavor. As A. K. Rogers says, "It is surely not man's sole business to find out which way the wind is blowing and then add his own breath to swell it. Every cause must once have been young; if it cannot gain adherents until it has already shown that it will succeed how is it ever to make a start?" [14] And as he further points out, the force of an ideal depends not on one's finding that it is an established fact, but on one's insistence that it shall be a fact.

It should also be borne in mind that the realist who disparages ideals is himself committed to certain ideals. The realist may be using a different terminology. Yet when objecting to a disturbing idealistic economic theory or political project he shows that it is his desire to preserve the *status quo,* which he regards

---

[14] *Ethics and Tolerance,* New York, Macmillan, 1934, pp. 59-60.

as beneficial. The conflict in him is really between one ideal and another.

Historically, the attitudes of the "idealists" and the "realists" have been interpreted in such a way as to make impossible any reconciliation between them. The idealist claims to stand for perfection, and the realist for the finality of brute facts. If these attitudes are not carried to extremes, both have something to offer for the realization of ideals. The idealist is right in insisting that one should not accept actualities as final and that one should look to the future for greater possibilities. The idealist is also right in insisting that actively pursuing an ideal is itself a factual element in the world. The realist on his part is right in maintaining that without an intelligent use of practical means, the pursuit of ideals is a futile activity. If we disire the actual progressive realization of our ideals, our aspirations must be shaped by a realistic understanding of the facts of human nature as well as of the world.

IV

There is one further issue. Though ideals have certain common aspects, they differ in their quality. In committing oneself to an ideal one has to examine and critically evaluate it. What are the criteria for evaluating ideals?

First, an ideal must have some firm roots in human nature. If one finds in himself the tendency to agree with general human aspirations, one has the right to infer that this tendency has some connection with man's normal constitution. Human desires and aspirations for knowledge, abundance, morality, and art have broad bases and long historic developments. There will always be deviations from the normal, but, by and large, what one aspires to is what other human beings aspire to.

Similarly, the major ideals of mankind must be desirable not only for a limited number of individuals or groups or for one particular culture, but for all mankind. The Greeks in formulating their larger objectives did not consider slaves as members of mankind; the Romans in pursuing their great political ambitions did not regard non-Romans as equals; similarly, many cultural and national groups in exalting their objectives did not consider the aspirations of other cultures or nations. In our day the West tends to ignore the East and the East the West in making their judgments of right or wrong, and both tend to ignore the possible attitudes of the generations to come.

An ideal must also have an immediate, personal appeal; the mere fact of popular agreement cannot be taken as a sufficient test for the validity of an ideal. The protestant is entitled to consideration. So long as we are in the process of groping after a human good the nature of which is still in dispute, we are necessarily dependent to a degree on our personal judgment. Resort to a majority judgment is always a risk.

Yet the personal testing of an ideal need not issue in discarding the previous one. The importance of common agreement does not lie in the mere number of those who hold an opinion but rather in its persistence through time, since such persistence tends to substantiate the opinion in question as an essential part of human nature.

Ideals must be pragmatically tested. Peace is a noble ideal, but dogmatic pacifism may have disastrous results. Liberty is a great ideal, but unlimited liberty may result in violence. Ideals must have a certain degree of stability, yet they must leave room for revision and modifications. Two extremes have to be avoided: the policy of drift with no guiding principle, and the retention of traditionally rigid ideals with no relevance to the present.

One final point. Since the realm of ideals is rich and varied, we can hardly claim that we have the final answer to human aspiration. In our pursuits there have to be broader visions and greater tolerance. Even the extreme demands of ideals that have failed have enriched human civilization — stoic endurance, Christian charity, romanticism, chivalry, scientism, revolutionary fanaticism — all of these despite their overdrawn assumptions have something admirable and engaging and tend to enlarge the thrust toward steadier ideals.

V

The nature of ideals has been analyzed and the tests for the desirable ones have been indicated. One final question, which was briefly mentioned earlier, needs to be stated. What common ideals should human beings pursue to attain something like real satisfaction? There are certain universal ideals that can be said to perform this function. First, there is the ideal of science. The knowledge we get from science not only satisfies our curiosity but proves to be an effective source of power. Secondly, there is the ideal of technology. The objective here is to apply our knowledge of science to productive means of security and abundance. Thirdly, since science and technology may be used for good as well as for evil, we need morality to direct them toward good ends only. Fourthly, we need art to sustain the human spirit with courage and broadening of perspectives. Finally, although science, technology, morality, and art are relatively independent, they are nevertheless closely interrelated. The integration of these ideals may be said to constitute a natural religion, the relatively ultimate objective of the human race.

The pursuit of these ideals, though necessary for human fulfillment, is not the whole of life. We need not ignore the satisfaction that comes from our daily pursuit of immediately attainable objectives. These, after all, constitute the bulk of our activities. And the ideals we mentioned must have vital relevance to daily activities. This relevance should not be ignored, but the rest of this discussion will be concerned with the ideals of science, technology, morality, art and religion.

Chapter IV

SCIENCE AND THE SEARCH FOR KNOWLEDGE

For human fulfillment knowledge is indispensable. For most elementary needs knowledge is a necessity. As human needs and aspirations increase, the demand for more knowledge increases. Knowledge is also a source of our enlightenment. To know ourselves and the kind of world we live in is a distinctive human desire.

I

Human beings have always sought ways of getting knowledge. This pursuit has not been easy. Deceptive leads, unreliable procedures, and unfounded beliefs have dissipated much effort. In the early periods of the human race, magic, soothsaying, astrology, and the assertiveness of political and religious authorities have been the dominant ways of knowledge. These ways, loaded with superstition, fear, and irrational beliefs had failed to fulfill the actual needs of knowledge. Yet primitive man despite all his magic and soothsaying possessed a great deal of empirical knowledge and knew something of the empirical way of solving problems. In everyday practical situations causal connections were observed. The uses of fire and of plants and the capture and domestication of animals were to some extent achieved, but the existent empirical knowledge did not give rise to significant generalizations.

From the early civilizations of Assyria, Babylon, Egypt, and Greece to the Medieval era, the search for dependable ways of knowledge had persisted. There was the authoritarianism of the religious and political leaders, the intuitionism of the mystics, and the somewhat more rational ways of the various practitioners and philosophers. The pursuit of reliable knowledge persisted in a more advanced and responsible way in the historic periods of rationalism and classic empiricism. These methods suggested important insights, but they were limited in scope.

Rationalism considered reason as the source of truth. Reason questioned old dogmas and unsupported beliefs; it classified problems on the basis of their essential elements and offered solutions by rigorous logical analysis. It was only natural that keen minds should have turned to reason as their guide in the search for knowledge.

What, then, is reason? The concept of reason, like other great concepts, had its evolution by way of varied meanings. For Plato reason was the faculty that comprehends the ultimate forms of things; for Aristotle it was that which grasped the essentials of diverse instances; for the Stoics it was elevated to cosmic significance, becoming not only reality but itself the nature of the whole reality.

Coming to the heyday of rationalism in the seventeenth century, reason for Descartes, Spinoza, and Leibnitz meant the rigorous demonstrations of mathematics. Truth in every area, even in morality, had to be established by this method. Spinoza tried to construct "ethics after the manner of a geometry." Out of all branches of mathematics geometry was chosen as the model for truth. Geometry dealt with propositions about the relations of points, lines, and surfaces. The premises from which geometric assertions were deduced are very simple, e.g., "All right angles are equal," or "A straight line is the shortest distance between two points." And these assertions in turn are deduced from equally simple formulas, like all A is A; nothing can be both A and not A; anything must be either A or not A; if all A is B, then some B is A; if all B is A and all C is B, then all C is A. These and similar logical and mathematical assertions were taken to be inexorable, though Descartes still had some doubts about them. If God is all powerful, we do not yet know, as Descartes thought, whether it might not be His will to create us so that we are always deceived. We believe "All right angles to be equal," though in truth they may not be.

Leibnitz was clearer on the nature of mathematical concepts. For Leibnitz the axioms of geometry were based upon the

Law of Identity, or what we call definitions. "A square is a four-sided figure"; we can have no doubt about this assertion since it is obviously our definition.

Gradually it becomes clear that logical and mathematical claims are purely analytic; they present consistent systems, but they can tell us nothing about the facts of the world. Definitions for reason far from being necessary propositions, are not propositions at all, but rather proposals; their rejection or acceptance can be neither true nor false. A triangle is a three-sided plane figure, but whether there is such a thing as a triangle one must discover by looking. Reason, though of great importance in the pursuit of knowledge, is not a sufficient guide for answering questions of fact.

The classic empiricists, in contrast to the rationalists, emphasized the importance of experience. Questions of fact had to be determined directly by experience. How do we know that the sun is shining, that fire is warming, that the rose has a pleasant odor except by seeing, touching, smelling? Empiricism had great appeal because of the common-sense maxim "seeing is believing."

Empiricism like rationalism had a long history. The Greek Sophists raised critical objections to the abstractions and artificialities of reason. To know, for them, was to perceive, and to perceive was to know. Protagoras's famous saying that "man is the measure of all things" emphasized the experimental aspect of knowledge.

The classic empiricists, like Locke, Berkeley, and Hume, clarified and strengthened the empirical claims of knowledge. Our knowledge of the world depends, for Locke, on two "fountains of experience." First, particular objects convey into the mind several distinct perceptions, and thus we come to have the ideas of *"yellow, white, heat, cold, hard, bitter, sweet,* and all those we call sensible qualities."[1] Secondly, there is the perception of the operations of the mind as it employs the ideas it has. These operations are *"perception, thinking, believing, doubting, reasoning, knowing, willing,* and all the different actings of our own minds."[2] Mind, for Locke, is wholly passive in

---

[1] *Essay Concerning Human Understanding,* Book II, Chapters 1-3.
[2] *Ibid.,* 4.

the reception of simple ideas; it exerts several acts of its own whereby out of its simple ideas others are framed.

That our knowledge has its roots in experience has to be accepted and must never be ignored; yet the classic empiricists' description of experience as well as their theory of knowledge was not satisfactory. What they called simple ideas turned out to be quite complex sensations of experience. Their description of knowledge had left no meaningful place for the mind's classification and naming of the experience. As Singer says, " 'Experience' is a name for our intellectual stride, it does not include in its meaning the foot-hold from which the stride swings off. . . . Before we are in any position to judge the hardness and fastness of the world of facts as experience reveals it to us, we must examine the nature of what is called—'*Bedingungen die die Erfahrung möglich machen*,' the conditions that make experience possible."[3]

With the growth of science, a major breakthrough occurred. In the scientific method, reason and experience were vitally interrelated and a verifiable, self-corrective procedure was developed. In the present essay, the method of science is accepted as the way of knowing in every area of human endeavor.

The beginning of science goes back many centuries. It is traditional to say that the Greeks created European science, but their achievement was founded on knowledge which had been inherited from earlier Babylonian and Egyptian civilizations. Greek civilization lost its creative power as ancient civilization decayed, but with the dawn of the modern era science emerged with new power. Vesalius's insistence upon dissection for anatomy, Galileo's experiments on falling bodies, Copernicus's and Kepler's astronomical theories, and finally Newton's mechanical image of nature gave great vitality to science. In the nineteenth century the Darwinian theory of evolution, and in the early part of our century Einstein's relativistic theory and Heisenberg's theory of quantum mechanics opened new horizons.

---

[3] *Experience and Reflection*, Philadelphia, U of Pa Pr, 1959, page 34. For a more detailed analysis of rationalism and classic empiricism see Chapters 2 and 3 in the same book.

II

Science has many different aspects, but its common core is its method of getting knowledge. Yet this method should not be described too narrowly. In the most general sense the scientific method is the best use of intelligence for a given problem, or, in other words, it is the most effective guide in the pursuit of knowledge. Just what is this method?

A creative scientist never follows the rigid routine of the scientific method as described by logicians. His activity is more imaginative and quite adventurous with many steps of trial and error. His pursuit of knowledge is quite different from the orderly manner in which he finally presents his results. Yet observing the activity of the scientists on a large scale one finds certain crucial steps.

There is, first of all, a problem to be investigated. This problem may come from an everyday observation or from a highly technical microscopic or macroscopic observation. The problems to be investigated cover wide areas of human interest. What is the pattern of the astronomical world? Why do seasons change? How does light travel? What is the structure of the atom? Are space and time absolute? What are the consequences of mixing different elements? Some scientists, curious about living beings and therefore watching plants and animals, were eager to discover the causes of growth, propagation, and heredity. Human curiosity also began asking questions about human behavior, social action, and historic processes.

Given the problem, the scientist, through hunches and gradually through some well-formulated hypothesis or theory, tries to arrive at a solution. There are no specific rules to obtain a fruitful hypothesis or theory, any more than there are specific rules to produce a work of art. Yet at every stage of an inquiry a hypothesis is required and it must be so stated that implications can be drawn from it.

What is a hypothesis, or, the more inclusive notion, a theory? There is no basic disagreement about the logical structure and general function of a theory; but there is wide disagreement about its cognitive nature. The complex analysis of this issue will not be gone into, yet the generally acknowledged view should be stated. Scientific theories, not unlike products of art, are imaginative creations; they are inventions of ingenious scientific minds. Scientific theories are not photographic descriptions of facts; they are creative organizations of facts. There is thus a distinction between so-called observable facts and the stipulations, classifications, and theories to which they are subjected by the mind. So-called facts may be independent of some classification, but not of all classifications. Even the facts to be classified are the resultant of some prior classification. The examination of the operational functioning of science shows that the scientist has a certain degree of choice in his theories. The Copernican picture of the solar system is different from the Ptolemaic one, and was the result of a creative act of the imagination. This choice was not based on new observation, but was between two antecedently presented images that were analytically connected, and Copernicus decided to pass from one to the other by a specific transformation. Similarly, Newton's great achievement was also the result of imaginative choice. His choice was between a great number of possible laws falling within the probable errors of his data. Newton by basing his thought on the separate inductions of Galileo and Kepler was able to formulate a single law that was close to theirs but not identical with them. And, again, the Einsteinian theory that space and time are relative was the result of choice between alternative descriptions. In a sense scientific theories are "arbitrary." This does not mean that they are capricious, but only that they result from a choice, and from a choice that is guided by the ideals of science, such as simplicity, comprehensiveness, and primarily pragmatic productivity.

Scientific theories, especially in their advanced stage, are highly abstract. Their relevancy to everyday qualitative events may not seem obvious, yet they are intended to explain them. Abstractions do not necessarily deny the qualities or values of our common world. Science begins within the matrix of our common world and comes back to it. What scientific theories are concerned with is not the denial of the qualities or values of events, but with the determination of the conditions under

which events are generated. The occurrence of a color—say blue—
depends on certain physical conditions, on electro-dynamic vibrations of a certain wavelength; in determining these conditions
one does not reduce the color blue to electro-dynamic vibrations.
As Ernest Nagel says, ". . . the unusually abstract character of
scientific notions, as well as their alleged 'remoteness' from the
traits of things found in customary experience, are inescapable
concomitants of the quest for systematic and comprehensive explanation."[4] To achieve generality for qualitatively diverse
things, "structural properties must be formulated without reference to, and in abstraction from, the individualizing qualities
and relations of familiar experience."[5]

It should also be noted that the scientific hypotheses or
theories are predictive. No theory can win acceptance unless it
makes prediction possible. Science is concerned with so describing
the passing events that their future can be predicted and controlled. Yet prediction should not be construed in too narrow
a sense. Prediction is based on our knowledge that if certain
conditions occur certain events will happen. In the advanced
sciences the predictive theories are described by precise mathematical, quantitative formulas in the interest of precise prediction.

The cumulative knowledge of science is not committed to
dogmatism. What science says about nature is continually modified. In physics, in biology, in psychology, in the social sciences,
the frontiers are changing. Recent theories in physics—the relativity theory and the theory of quantum mechanics—have greatly
modified former notions of space, time, causality, and matter.
Similarly, in biology new theories of heredity and in psychology
a truer analysis of human behavior and in anthropology an
intenser study of comparative cultures have significantly transformed our ideas of life, mind, and society. The more we explore
the depths of nature, the more unsuspected facts and laws we
discover. The basic principles of science as well as its verified
facts are not incorrigible. What establishes the claim of scientific
knowledge is the method of evaluating evidence for a particular

---

[4] *The Structure of Science*, New York, H B & W., 1961, p. 11.
[5] *Ibid.*, p. 11.

claim. This method is self-corrective and is always open to further inquiry.

A final word about the ideal of science. Although the scientist approaches his problems with some prior knowledge, this knowledge is provisional and corrigible. In the light of new evidence, new methods of measurement, and new theories the prior knowledge is modified. Questions of science are never settled with absolute certainty, yet the scientists have the deeply rooted belief that there must be answers to their questions. The ideal of science is to find better and better solutions to their problems—solutions that are errorless. This ideal of scientific progress can only be approached. Earlier a distinction was drawn between objectives and ideals; the former are attainable but the latter are essentially unattainable though indefinitely approachable.

III

Scientific knowledge has been the dominant achievement of the modern era, yet there have been certain objections to its validity and scope. Three of these will be referred to. First, there is the claim that because scientific knowledge is abstract it cannot give us the knowledge of the unique, historic, and value aspects of experience. Secondly, it has been maintained that science is mechanistic and so fails to explain the teleological processes of life and mind. Finally, it has been maintained that scientific knowledge is limited in scope, whereas the metaphysical conception of reality as mind or spirit goes beyond science and gives us a more ultimate explanation.

There have been a number of objections to the so-called abstractness of scientific knowledge. It has been maintained that it fails to give us knowledge of the concrete, historic, unique, qualitative events. Fechner calls the abstract image of nature the "night view of nature"—a qualityless, purposeless, cause-tight nature. Many theologians and philosophers have expressed similar views. For James Ward, one of the major critics of the naturalistic philosophy in the early twenties, it is history not science which can give us reality in its concreteness. "With the experience in the concrete, we can deal satisfactorily in no other way,

and no competent thinker dreams of interpreting the history of
the world by means of a scheme of universal laws."[6] In history,
the claim is, we find no mere repetition or fixity and therefore
it is not subject to exact measurement or mathematics. What we
find in the world of history are facts, individuals, progress or
decline—all of which we miss in the world of science. Thus the
world of science and the world of history have little or nothing
in common; "their terminology, their categories, their problems
are wholly different."[7] For Josiah Royce there is a separation,
though not so sharp, between the World of Description and the
World of Appreciation. ". . . were our human intercourse of
another sort, were all the moments of all our human lives directly
appreciable by us together and at our pleasure . . . *then,*" as Royce
claims, "the world of our accessible truth would have quite another aspect from that of the world of description."[8] Scientific
description, though necessary, is inadequate. In order "to make
our description valid for all intelligent human beings, the fash-
ions of our description have to be universal. We can't describe
the unique, e.g., Shelley's 'sense that at the winds of spring,' etc.
That we have to appreciate."[9]

William Hocking, similarly, though he does not discard a
limited use of the abstract universals of science, maintains that
the abstractions of science give us the "night view" of nature.
Science deprives nature "not alone of all purpose in the shape
of 'final causes,' but as well of all quality and value."[10] From the
scientific standpoint the cosmos we live in is purposeless and
devoid of qualities; it is a realm of fact and event ideally mathematical in structure and process, ideally devoid of meaning.
Science in its zeal has made or has implied metaphysical assertions
to which it has no right, that nature mathematically conceived is
the whole of reality, that what empirical science can show is the
only acceptable truth, that what the science of man can show of
man is the whole of man.

---

6 *Naturalism and Agnosticism,* New York, Macmillan, 1899, Vol. II, p. 280.

7 *Realm of Ends,* Cambridge, Cambridge U Pre, 1911, p. 2.

8 *The Spirit of Modern Philisophy,* Boston and New York, H M., 1892, p. 395.

9 *Ibid.,* p. 398.

10 *The Coming World Civilization,* New York, Harper & Brothers, 1956, p. 55.

The claim that science as mere abstraction and description never gives us real knowledge and that history as knowledge of the unique or the individual presents a genuine insight into reality is not a well-founded doctrine. It may be granted that existing beings, animate and inanimate, are individuals, concrete and unique. This assumption, however, should not lead to a sharp dualism between the historic and the scientific types of knowledge. Despite certain important differences between these two types of knowledge there is fundamental identity. A successful attack on one of them would be quite fatal to the other.

Abstractions neither distort nor limit our knowledge. All cognitive activities make selections and distinctions unless cognition is identified merely with an intensive reduplication of experience. All significant assertions about the individual or the concrete are in terms of universals or abstractions. Take any historical event which is individual, unique and unrepeatable, such as the invasion of Russia by Napoleon; each incident and happening in this campaign, such as Napoleon's march through Poland, his encounter with the Russians at Borodino, the setting of Moscow on fire by the Russians before Napoleon's entrance, the enormous loss of men in the campaign—all of these events though unique and unrepeatable can nevertheless be described in terms of concepts and universals. Apart from universals such as "encounter," "fire," "entrance," "loss," terms which are applicable to many situations, the understanding of these unique events would be impossible. The proposition that reality is historic, individual, and concrete should not be identified with the untenable doctrine that the individual is real apart from any concepts or abstractions.

As a matter of fact, scientific knowledge, which is allegedly discredited because of its abstractions, does not dispense with the concrete or the individual or the value. The aim of natural science is to understand the nature of the actual world, and not to construct the laws of all possible worlds. The geologist who is trying to determine and analyze the various stages of the evolution of the earth is dealing with something which is specific, unique and individual. The incidents here are almost as unrepeatable as Napoleon's Russian campaign. In a more limited sense, the same thing is true of the physicist, the biologist, and the psychologist. As Morris R. Cohen says, ". . . every physicist in the laboratory as well as the engineer engaged in testing a bridge or particular engine is engaged with an individual object."[11] The scientist is, undoubtedly, trying to understand laws, invariant relations, and the causal connections between events. This fact, however, should not lead one to the belief that the scientist has no concern with the individual or the concrete. The laws which are discovered are laws of specific realms of existence.

Finally, though scientific knowledge is abstract, the abstractions do not in any way deny the qualities or values of events. Science starts from our sensuous experience, our feelings and desires, and formulates relevant hypotheses or theories and then returns to our daily experience. Science is not concerned with the denial of qualities or values, but with the determination of the conditions under which these experiences are generated.

The second objection to science is that it is mechanistic in outlook and therefore unable to explain the purposive processes of life and mind. The issue here is not merely between abstraction and concreteness but between mechanism and teleology. Before stating the nature of the controversy it will be necessary to clarify the notion of mechanism. Mechanism has a strict and a looser meaning. In the strict sense it means explanation in terms of the basic concepts of mechanics; but in its looser sense it means explanation in terms of physicochemical concepts. Usually it is in the latter sense that life and mind are meant to be mechanistic.

The controversy between mechanism and teleology has a long history, extending from the days of Democritus and Aristotle to the present time. There are many different types of objection to mechanism in biology and psychology, but the clearest and the most forceful objections are those of the vitalists and the dualists. Their central claim is that living beings and mental beings are more than physicochemical systems and that this something more is a nonperceptible, nonmechanical agency like entelechy, élan

---

[11] *Reason and Nature*, H B & W., 1931, p. 14.

vital, or spirit. It is one of these agencies that is the guiding force
of purposive activities.

The arguments for vitalism and dualism are numerous and
complex. For H. Driesch, a leading vitalist of the recent past,
organic form, organic growth, organic action demand entelechy.
His first argument especially caused considerable discussion.
According to him morphogenetic systems are "harmonious equi-
potential systems," that is to say, each of their elements may play
every single part of the totality of what will occur in the whole
system.[12] This, he claims, cannot be explained mechanistically,
but needs entelechy to account for it. For Bergson mechanism
would be refuted if "it could be proved that life may manufacture
the like apparatus by unlike means on divergent lines of evolution."[13] He uses as example the eye of a vertebrate and the
eye of a mollusc, the latter of a common Pecten. Whence the
structural analogy? To solve the difficulty he suggests the
hypothesis that élan vital, finding itself opposed by matter, makes
an effort to overcome the obstacles and does this by an indi-
visible act. The result is the visual apparatus. The arguments
offered by the dualists are similar in principle to those of the
vitalists. Perception, memory, meaning, and the results of psychical research are all used as arguments against mechanism. The
central claim is that mental events are psychical or spiritual in
nature with no physical counterpart.

Certain central remarks are relevant in regard to what the
vitalists and the dualists claim.

First, the vitalistic and the dualistic agencies like entelechy,
élan vital, and anima are not open to empirical investigation;
they are unverifiable. Entelechy, e.g., is neither "substance" nor
"attribute" nor "quantity." Driesch gives the impression that
it is not even in space. It is true that in science there were entities
which were recognized and used as a basis for explanation long
before they were verified or isolated. Similar entities, however,
were isolated, and the verification of the entities which were not

---

12 *Science and Philosophy of Organism,* London, A & C Black Co., 1908, Vol. I,
pp. 120-1.

13 *Creative Evolution,* Trans. Arthur Mitchell, New York, Henry Holt & Co., 1911,
pp. 54-55.

isolated presented only varying degrees of difficulty. Entelechy, or anything like entelechy, has never been isolated; hence, as C. B. Broad says, "entelechy is a purely hypothetical entity in a sense in which an as yet unisolated but suspected chemical element is not."[14] And the reason why entelechy is unverifiable may be its nonexistence.

Secondly, these suggestions do not in any way relieve the difficulties involved. The arguments raised by vitalists and dualists poise mostly difficulties which are gradually being met by nonvitalistic explanation. The vitalistic agencies solve the problems by creating more difficult problems. Driesch's entelechy is endowed with miraculous knowledge, prior to any experience, about the whole process of the organic and inorganic realms. Bergson's élan vital is similarly miraculous. If élan vital by invisible act can accomplish all the things Bergson is claiming, then one may as well give up the attempt to understand the happenings of evolution. And the claim of dualists like Bergson and McDougall that psychological activities have no physiological correlate has not been proven. One could accept, e.g., the difficulties mentioned by Bergson without resorting to his implication that memory must be independent of natural mechanism. Because certain lesions do not destroy memory it does not follow that certain additional lesions would not destroy it. Memory may be independent of several neural mechanisms, but not of all neural mechanisms. Similarly, McDougall's claim that meaning demands a psychic relating agency is not the only alternative. As Lloyd Morgan says, "May not the relating activity, so-called, be just as reasonably assigned to the physiological process in the cortex and the organism as a whole as to the correlated psychological process, hypothesized as a psychic entity?"[15]

One need not assume that mechanism and teleology are incompatible. By arguing for the universal applicability of mechanism, I do not claim that mechanism presents a complete, exhaustive understanding of existence. It is the claim of the mechanists that this is the case. This belief I do not entertain. Mechanism

---

[14] *The Mind and Its Place in Nature,* London, Kegan Paul, Trench, Trubner & Co., 1925, p. 57.

[15] *Instinct and Experience,* London, Methuen & Co., 1912, p. 280.

is not the only basic classification. There is the possibility of a number of such basic classifications. Life, and one could add mind, should be defined in terms of purpose.

Empirically, life and mind are manifestations of the processes of nature. Life and mind occur at a certain level of complexity in the physicochemical, organic structure. This assumption neither denies nor belittles the specific properties of life and mind. What this assumption requires is, first, a careful analysis of the physicochemical, organic processes at the basis of life and mind, and, second, a careful description of the specific traits which mental beings exhibit, such as adaptation, sensation, feeling, thinking, willing. All these traits can be described experimentally and naturalistically.

One can agree with the vitalists that in describing the nature of life and mind we should not deny their purposive activities, but one must equally insist that these activities are natural processes. For certain purposes the actions of living and human beings may be described in causal terms, but for other purposes their observable behavior may be described without reference to causal conditions but in relation to ends or goals. These two types of explanation are consistent, equally useful, and equally experimental. What is suggested here is what in principle we all accept in describing time-pieces; we may either examine their mechanical structure, as that of the sundial, watch, or chronoscope, or indicate their function without considering their mechanical structure.

The third objection to science is based on the claim that reality is Mind or Spirit and that science at its best cannot fathom the ultimate nature of the world. This view has a long history and many variations and many subtle arguments. One of the central arguments of the modern idealists has been the epistemological one. This argument asserts that the knower or mind is primary, whereas the known object is derivative, dependent on the mind and ultimately on a universal mind.

The epistemological argument consists of two parts. First, it is argued, in Berkelian fashion, that the external objects depend on mind for existence. By various devices it is argued that the world of our knowledge, whatever it be, is through and through of the stuff that ideas are made of, that anything that is definable is an idea, that, as Berkeley puts it, "this whole choir of heaven and furniture of earth is nothing for any of us but a system of ideas which govern our belief and conduct." What do we mean, Royce asks, by the shape of anything or by the size of anything? What is the meaning of any property that we give to the outer world? All these, he maintains, can be expressed only in terms of ideas. What, for instance, are trees or mountains but sensations of mind, and what are sound waves or other waves but conceptions of mind to explain the facts of nature?[16]

The argument so far merely attempts to establish the claim that external objects depend for their existence on mind; the reality of the Supreme Mind has not yet been proved. To find this proof we must pass to the second part of the idealist's argument. As Royce maintains, our knowledge always looks beyond the immediate present. He says, "I am always meaning to inquire into objects beyond me." How do we recognize the objects in our environment if not by combining our preception of them with memories of them as perceived in the past? How do we recall a forgotten name if not with memories of it as perceived in the past? How do we recall a forgotten name if not by appealing to our larger self of memory which knows the name? In knowledge, Royce argues, we must always draw more on a larger self than on the immediate one. Again, how do we settle our arguments? There must be some common framework for arriving at the truth. To escape conflict of aims or the relativity of human ideas, we must assume a self-consistent system of ideas, and this system is, for Royce, our Deeper Self or the Absolute.

Similarly, Hocking argues that to escape from the limitations of our individual lives into the full meaning of life and to establish anchorage in reality we must attain a "personal intimacy of the whole." The Whole, for Hocking, is the ultimate independent being on which other things depend. The Whole is in a sense other than Nature, myself, and my fellow beings, yet it includes all these in so far as they are its created work. The Whole, as the

---

[16] *The Spirit of Modern Philosophy*, Boston and New York, H M., 1892, Chapter XI.

Absolute Self, gives meaning and value to existence. Meaning and value are mere abstractions if independent of the mind; they can only be intelligible in relation to the Absolute Self. The mere factual aspect of things acquires rationality only when viewed and organized in the context of the Whole. Because man as metaphysician is "concerned with the real, he is bound to be concerned with the Whole."[17] Neither the human mind nor the human will can be content with only a part of reality; to aspire to union with the Whole is a characteristically human trait.[18]

The central contention of the epistemological interpretation is, as mentioned earlier, the claim that the knower, or mind, is primary, whereas the object known is derivative, being dependent on mind. Apart from mind, it is asserted, the physical world has no independent reality. Omitting for the present the emotional considerations, the reason for this assertion is the fact that the object known is always related to the mind, and that apart from this relation there is no knowledge. From the obvious fact that in the knowing process the object known is related to mind the inference is drawn that the object of knowledge depends on mind. The idealist's claim is a pure dogma, and his inference is the result of a confusion of concepts. To be related does not necessarily mean to be dependent on. It is true that in certain cases, such as in error or illusion, the object of knowledge has a twofold relation to mind, viz., it is related to mind as an object to a subject, and it is dependent upon mind for its existence. To jump from this to the conclusion that *all* that is related to mind is therefore dependent on mind is a fallacious conversion. An object may be related to mind and yet have existence independent of that relation. R. B. Perry has felicitously called this fallacy "the egocentric predicament." We never escape the fact that the object known is always related to mind—this is the "egocentric predicament"; but this fact in no sense proves that the object known has no existence apart from this relation, or that there

---

17 Metaphysics: its function, consequences and criteria, *The Journal of Philosophy*, Vol. *XLIII*, July 4, 1946, p. 372.

18 For a fuller discussion of Hocking, see the present writer's "Hocking and the dilemmas of modernity," in *The Journal of Philosophy*, Vol. *LV*, No. 7, 1958, and Hocking's rejoinder in the same issue.

are no other objects which are not in the knowledge relation to ourselves or to other minds.

As for the second argument, the universal Self is involved in difficulties. Reality is incurably pluralistic and contingent. We never face the universal Self that the idealist is concerned with. There are relative systems like the molecule, the organism, the family, and the state, but the universal Self as one integrated meaningful totality is not within our experience. At best such an idea of totality may be considered as a regulative whole for the scientist. Nature may be taken as the ideal of completed science. But here the idea of the whole is an ideal limit that one may approach but never reach.

Empirically mind is a latecomer. Should one entertain the theory of evolution as an actual process, there should be no difficulty in considering life and mind as later emergencies. Empirically mind is only one thing among many other results of the evolutionary process and as transient and perishable as some of the other important results of evolution.

IV

The method of science to obtain knowledge has been defined, and some of the objections to scientific knowledge have been examined. What must now be considered is the value of science to man. Just how is science a source of human fulfillment? There are two aspects of science which are important in the pursuit of a satisfactory life—understanding and control. These two aspects are vitally interrelated, yet each has its distinctive contributions.

First, as to understanding. Scientific knowledge has intrinsic value for human beings. Despite the present emphasis on the usefulness of knowledge one may pursue knowledge for the experience of sheer enlightenment. One may even become a devotee of truth and so enrich one's world of values. Knowledge of the vast astronomical world, of the intricate microscopic world of atoms, of the organic evolution of living beings, of the behavior of human beings, of the origin and growth of civilization—these kinds of knowledge are among the most satisfying possessions of man.

And scientific knowledge being rational, it satisfies the human demand for reliable knowledge. Scientific knowledge is rational not merely in the analytic sense of reason, but in the sense that its rationality is deeply rooted in human nature. Even in the most primitive societies there are attempts to get dependable knowledge. Scientific knowledge as rational, evidential knowledge is applicable not only to the physical and biological world but to other areas of human activity. Human beings are hampered by ill-founded beliefs in their racial, political, economic, ethical, and religious pursuits. Science approaches these pursuits with the same dependable rationality.

Scientific knowledge is also universalistic. What is true for me is true for all. The mathematical and physical theories taught in America and in China are the same. Should we learn to study politics, history, or religion, all nations would have a common basis for understanding in these areas. Scientific knowledge is open to all men. As Bernard Barber says, in discussing the "community of scientists and scholars." "This is a community of moral partners, and its reach is beyond the national group; science is international, it is universal in its ideal."[19] The universality of science does not eliminate individual judgment, individual thinking, individual errors. But since the basis of scientific knowledge is evidential, attention is given to what is common rather than to what divides man. Scientific hypotheses are established by intersubjective confirmation and not by isolated claims.

Scientific knowledge is a cooperative enterprise; it has world wide collaboration. Potentially all men are eligible for the scientific pursuit. Though professional scientists form a class, this class does not recognize color, nation, or race. And one's scientific contribution is usefully shared by others. The developments in mathematics help the physicists; and those in physics help the chemists and biologists. And a free, enlightened social milieu helps all scientists.

The second value of science is that it controls events. "Knowledge is power." And power is one of our deepest desires. As E. Singer says, "Is there anything that anyone could wish to

---

[19] *Science and the Social Order,* New York, Collier Books, p. 128.

have, but that he must, at the very same time, wish he had more power than he has to achieve that thing? Surely, all desirous beings, conscious enough to reflect upon their state, must recognize in themselves the eternal desire for greater power, greater control over events, greater emancipation from fate, heightened probability of achievement, lessened probability of defeat."[20]

The belief that through science we can make our way through difficulties and dangers is based on the idea that a cause discovered is a cause controlled. The principle of causality—strict or statistical—cannot be established by pure reason or by pure empirical evidence; yet it has been a most useful guiding principle. The control of events for human progress through a knowledge of causal relations is distinctively a modern idea. The Greeks and Romans were on the whole of the opinion that the fundamental nature of things is fixed once and for all. There were changes, to be sure, but they were cyclical rather than progressive.

The notion of progress through science has been a widespread belief throughout the modern period. It found impressive expression in the writings of Francis Bacon in the early part of the seventeeth century; men like Turgot, Condorcet, and Priestley were similarly expressive on this subject in the eighteenth century; French socialists like Saint Simon and Faurier carried it to extravagant lengths in the early nineteenth century; Auguste Comte in France and John Stewart Mill, Thomas Huxley, Herbert Spencer and others in England disseminated this kind of philosophy in the middle of the nineteenth century; finally Charles Darwin's great theory of organic evolution gave it tremendous intellectual impetus in the latter part of the nineteenth century.

But the grip of the idea of progress through science is not due so much to the philosophers and prophets of progress as it is to the great development of the sciences, and above all to the amazing triumphs of applied science or technology. What must now be considered is the bearing of technology on human fulfillment.

---

[20] *In Search of A Way of Life*, New York, Columbia U Pr, 1948, p. 12.

Chapter V

TECHNOLOGY AND HUMAN WELFARE

Man is an active being; he pursues ends and struggles to attain them. In his pursuit he seeks means and instrumentalities to attain his ends. Technology, in its inclusive sense, is the source of means for ends. Technology has a long history. In its early period the available means for human needs were fire, hunting tools, and primitive devices for gathering food; at a later stage, agricultural developments; in the modern era, mechanical industrial inventions; and currently electricity, automation, and cybernetics. But technology is not limited to tools, machines, or automation; technique is also used in the organizational structure of the economic, political, military and other forms of human institutions. Technology may thus be defined as the means or the technique invented and used for the fulfillment of any human purpose whatsoever. In recent years the technological emphasis has been on automation and cybernetics.

The ideal of technology is to attain the most efficient productive means to fulfill human needs and desires; food, shelter, health, wealth, every type of social organization, economic, political, military, and educational. The technological ideal, like all ideals, is never fully attainable, though continually approachable.

I

Technology faces many difficult problems; some are technical, others, and the most disturbing ones, are social. For the present, assuming that these problems will be solved more or less adequately, it should be possible to indicate the benefits of technology.[1]

---

[1] For an enlightening discussion on technology, see Ayers, C. E., *Towards A Reasonable Society*, Austin, University of Texas, 1961, Chapters X-XV.

The first benefit is security. Insecurity is a major disturbing factor in human experience, so the search for security is universally desirable. There are many causes of anxiety over lack of security — inadequate food, disease, war, ambition, love, ennui. Current existentialism has given dramatic expression to various forms of insecurity.

There are different ways of meeting insecurity. One way has been an appeal to a Higher Power for help. This has been the method of the traditional religions. Another way of meeting insecurity has been through intelligence and the use of technology. There are, of course, certain forms of insecurity, such as the sense of the inevitable final destruction of life, which cannot be met by technological means, but the basic needs of human security, such as adequate food, the cure of disease, and the prevention of war are most effectively met by technological developments.

With regard to food it is quite evident that from the earliest time to our own era security has been achieved through technology. Primitive tools were the means of getting and accumulating food; agricultural revolution changed jungles to rich sources of food. In most countries the hazards of famine have been effectively met. Through large-scale technological organization localized abundance has been widely distributed, and regional failures have received the necessary help.

Similarly, the growth in our knowledge of chemistry, biology, physiology, and anatomy and the technical developments in medicine and the growth of hospitals have greatly alleviated the threat of disease and increased the means of cure. The production and distribution of therapeutic means for use in general practice, the availability of drugs and vaccines, and the supervision of communities by public health authorities have contributed immensely to communal health.

War is also a major cause of human insecurity. Technological developments have accelerated rather than diminished this cause of insecurity and the anxiety it gives rise to. Technological ingenuities have created such powerful weapons and means of destruction that human civilization and even human existence on this planet is in danger of extinction. We cannot minimize our present anxiety. Yet two points are worth mentioning. The danger of nuclear war is not solely the result of technological developments, though these have made such a war possible; violent national antagonisms and the traditional reliance on war are even more responsible. War is a cultural phenomenon and has therefore to be approached with psychological and sociological understanding. The very possibility of peace depends to a great degree on world organization, which in turn demands skillful social technique. And the fact that technological developments have a powerful drift towards universality is also conducive to peace.

Technological revolutions have brought greater security in most areas of human life, yet it is also true that these changes have brought new risks or insecurities. Technological forces may eventually bring disaster and destruction to the human race, but this is not inevitable. Human beings may still learn to achieve the benefits of technology without its sinister possibilities.

Security is a major concern of society, yet it cannot be regarded as absolute. There are other values than security. In our world there will always be risks. Human beings love risks and adventures even though their actions may have no immediate relevance to security or utility, like climbing high mountains, exploring new countries, and landing on the moon. There is an important difference between security and risk, between conservation and creation. Extreme security against hazards does not necessarily lead to achievements, it may even be detrimental. A world without risks would be intolerable. If there were no risks, human beings would create them. It is not the absence of risks that is desirable, but rather of such risks as are altogether unmanageable or meaningless.

Another benefit of technology is abundance. Abundance is more than having the minimum necessities for security; the excess makes possible a higher standard of living. At present, especially in this country, the resources and the means of production are sufficient to afford a high degree of satisfaction to the whole nation.

But neither our economic structure nor our traditional out-look on life has freed us from the philosophy of scarcity. To keep our present economic structure we dissipate and destroy our abundance; to keep our philosophy of scarcity we hesitate to make full use of our opportunity. When industrial efficiency produces an abundance that threatens to upset the established social order, the traditional social values require that it be resisted. We are so obsessed with the philosophy of scarcity that our industrial energies "must go to the creation of a cake which of necessity must grow and grow and never be cut." Keynes called this growth of the cake "the object of true religion." Yet the only justification for having the cake, as C. E. Ayers rightly points out, is to cut it. Instead of guiding our lives by the wisdom of scarcity we should learn to guide it by the wisdom of abundance.

One further point. There is the fear that because abundance emphasizes quantity it may lower quality. There is some justification for this fear. In many areas quantity has destroyed quality, but this need not happen. There is no inherent necessity that quantity should destroy quality. Because many more enjoy the music of Bach, Beethoven, and Brahms or are acquainted with the paintings of Titian, Leonardo DaVinci, and Reubens, or read Homer, Milton, and Goethe, or appreciate the scientific theories of Newton, Heisenberg, and Einstein, it does not follow that these great achievements need be lowered in estimation. There is a common belief that what is shared by many cannot be good. This is prejudice.

Still another benefit of technology is equality. Abundance is an agent of equality; the natural consequence of abundance is the steady reduction of poverty.

In all ages inequality has been the accepted pattern of society. This pattern has been maintained by tradition, myths, and social structure. In most civilizations it has been taken to be an unalterable fact that the "poor shall always be with us." The Egyptian, Greek, and Roman civilizations had their slaves; the Middle Ages had their serfs; modern industrial society has its laborers. Yet the ideal of equality has always been alive.

What precisely do we mean by equality? Equality is opposed

to arbitrary distinctions of rank, class, nationality, and race. It does not mean the absence of individual physical and mental differences; it simply means the absence of barriers to growth or, more positively, that everyone ought to have the opportunity for growth.

Technological advancement is making possible a more nearly equalitarian society. There are, certainly, great economic differences in our society, and it is possible to use technological forces to favor certain individuals. But there is the real possibility, which the human race had never had before, that through the productive means of technology a more equalitarian society may emerge. In an era of abundant housing, food, medical care, education, and traveling facilities, security is bound to be more widely shared.

Leisure is still another benefit of technology. Here we come to one of the most difficult problems of our technological civilization. Technology, especially cybernetics, is progressively displacing labor. This phenomenon has been observed by many and hardly needs statistical proof. What is not sufficiently realized is that this process is not reversible. No palliatives are adequate to meet this situation. As Alice Hilton points out, "electronic slaves" are invading the labor world. Displacement in wide areas is irresistible. And this displacement is occurring not only by firing laborers but more drastically by not hiring them. The considerable displacement of white-collar workers is steadily increasing. And, higher positions in big concerns are being replaced more and more by fewer professional technicians. Finally, cybernetics is replacing the functions provided by man's brain. In our productive system man is becoming obsolete. And as the new generation begins to flood the market for positions, the crisis will be intensified.

Since the further development of cybernetics will further increase the number of unemployed, it is obvious that eventually a large number of human beings will not be needed for any form of labor whatsoever. We shall soon face an era of great leisure. How will this amount of leisure be handled? There are two alternatives. Leisure may lead to a boring existence and the gradual disintegration of human worth, or it may lead to a fruitful, creative existence. The latter would make possible a highly satisfactory civilization.

II

As is apparent, technology can prove very beneficial, yet it can be highly destructive of human welfare. Technology is a neutral, amoral power; it thus may be used for either good or evil. What we must resolve to observe is that there are certain internal tendencies in technology which if not controlled will prove destructive. Some of these tendencies have already been referred to, but they should be stated more explicitly.

There is the ever-present problem in technology of the ends and means relation. One cannot, of course, too sharply separate ends from means; what is an end in one relation may be a means in another relation; similarly, what is a means in one relation may be an end in another relation. As has been often observed, there is continuity between ends and means. And yet there is an overall end in the use of technology that should be emphasized. Technology has no intrinsic value of its own, its value lies in relation to human desires and satisfactions. Yet there is always a drift in technological developments to overlook this valuable end.

Often technical progress pursues efficiency without any regard to human consequences. In many cases the search is solely for the best technical means. Human beings participate in technological growth, but their participation tends to focus on mere efficiency. For cars to travel efficiently roads are made without regard to what damage is done to the countryside; industrial plants are centralized and decentralized for the sole purpose of efficiency; and systems of production are created with the sole objective of improvement in method. As Jacques Ellul says, "Technique itself, *ipso facto* and without indulgence or possible discussion, selects among the means to be employed. The human being is no longer in any sense the agent of choice. . . . He does not make a choice of complex and, in some way, human motives. He can decide only in favor of the technique that gives maximum efficiency. But this is not choice."[2] Ellul's observations on the present technological preoccupation with efficiency are valid, yet one need not accept his belief that this drift is inevitable. Man may come to realize that technological progress should focus on human welfare and not on efficiency as a self-sufficient end.

And technology being an organizational activity, may also be carried to such extremes as to become detrimental to human welfare. Technology, especially in its economic, political, social, and administrative forms, emphasizes organization. That organization can bring many benefits through the combination and co-ordination of individual and group activities is to be admitted, but obsession with organization has its dangers. Extreme organization tends to create an impersonal, mechanized society. Individual ingenuities and spontaneities are sacrificed to standardized methods. Every movement is externally guided, every decision is made for the individual. Privacy of life is also endangered. In a tightly organized society every individual is tabulated, every activity is classified. Every aspect of privacy is recorded for possible future use. Life in such a society may become smooth, efficient, and comfortable, but basically insipid.

Technology also tends towards centralization. In an over-centralized society economic and political power and significant decisions will be limited more and more to a privileged group. In the rapidly cybernating society decision-making is more and more dependent on information from computers, and this is "privileged information." The final say seems to belong to the technical elites. In such a society most citizens may become marginal. This of course need not be the pattern of technological civilization, yet there is a powerful drift in this direction.

What are the conditions that would make technology a means of human welfare? Many of the disturbing technological problems have to be solved by technologists, yet there are certain general conditions which concern us all. Two of these will be mentioned.

If technological developments are to prove beneficial to society, the ideal of the democratically oriented industrial society

---

[2] *The Technological Society,* New York, Alfred A. Knopf, 1964, p. 80.

must be kept alive. Unless this ideal is realized as the guiding principle of technological benefits our society may easily drift towards a militarized, cybernated totalitarianism. Actions, and especially actions on a large scale, have far-reaching social consequences. If these consequences are conceived solely in relation to the profit and power of a limited group, technological production will not be a basic benefit to human society. Technology itself must try to solve the problem of a larger participation in the making of important decisions. It is of the utmost importance that our technological development be democratically controlled. The fruits of technology belong to all; they are the results of the ingenuity and scientific creativity of many individuals and nations. Technological abundance must be for the benefit of the human race and not for a limited class. There will, of course, always be unresolved social conflicts, but the ideal of technological productivity must be that of a cooperative civilization.

The second condition to make technology a means of human welfare is a new orientation to the philosophy of abundance. Certain basic ideals are more or less universal and permanent— freedom, justice, and human dignity—but there are certain large life-perspectives which are relative and relevant to different eras. For many generations the philosophy of scarcity was the dominant and necessary outlook on life. When jungles and forests had to be cleared, and the earth to be plowed, and the new countries to be developed the Biblical precept "Thou shalt eat thy bread in the sweat of thy face" was the necessary and reasonable conception, but in a technological civilization this conception would be wholly detrimental. We have to develop a philosophy of abundance and leisure; we must learn to enjoy the great benefits of technology without yielding to its possible evils. There is the potentiality of a new era in which the great mass of human beings can engage in the most satisfying creative activities.

Chapter VI

MORALITY AND THE STANDARDS OF ACTION

Science gives us knowledge, technology abundance. Knowledge and abundance are necessary conditions for a satisfactory life, but they are not sufficient. There are further issues of human conduct and human relations that have to be considered. What is the nature of the good life? How should one organize one's desires? How should one treat personal and social conflicts? Such and similar issues bring us to the realm of morality. And without morality human satisfaction is impossible.

Morality is the concern of all human beings. We are all involved in the issues of good and bad, right and wrong, justice and injustice, duty and prudence. Some moral problems are private and personal, others are public and social. At present the most pressing ones are global in scope.

Though moral issues are of paramount, universal importance, there is a great deal of confusion as to exactly what they are and how they should be approached. The traditionalists are absolutists and authoritarians in their view of morality. For them the standards of morality are given from above and our task is to follow these standards. The modernists are relativists and anti-authoritarians. For them there are no fixed universal standards of morality; moral precepts depend solely on individuals and groups. And there are also the extreme relativists, or amoralists, who would reject all standards of morality. For them morality in all its forms is considered a mode of repression and a sign of weakness; what count in the world are self-interest and power and not the principles of morality.

Our present moral dilemma may be stated thus: Morality demands common norms, universal standards for action; yet the drift of modern thought and events has been toward the rejection of such norms or standards. Relativistic morality is the dominant outlook of our era. Is there a way out of this dilemma? Can we meaningfully pursue moral ideals? In order to arrive at the resolution of this dilemma one must first know the logic and the trends that led to moral relativism.

I

For many generations Western civilization found its moral anchor in the Judeo-Christian conception. According to this conception, the world was created by God, and the moral order was imposed by His will. Morality meant acting in obedience to the will of God, and immorality meant acting in disobedience to His will. Moral laws were not made by man but by a supernatural agent. This view was dominant in the Middle Ages, and it is still the official doctrine of the major Christian Churches and, with some modifications, of the more liberal sectarian groups.

On a much more sophisticated level and addressed to smaller groups some philosophic systems also argue for absolutistic theories. Some of the absolutists base their claim on human intuition for what is good and what is right; others, like Kant, on categorical imperatives which are taken as universal laws; still others develop the notion of the Absolute, or the Universal Mind, as the source of moral values and standards. According to this latter conception, moral standards are not to be regarded as relative and man-made but as absolute and discovered by reason.

Beginning with the seventeenth century, a variety of trends, especially the development of the sciences, shook the foundations of the religious and philosophical defenses of the absolutistic standards of morality. There were, of course, many skeptics and critics of absolutistic morality in earlier periods. Yet these were comparatively minor strains in the history of relativistic morality. The major push toward relativism was to begin with the scientific revolution in the seventeenth century. Some of the major trends that have brought about moral relativism will now be indicated.

One major trend that ushered in moral relativism was the development of physical science in the seventeenth century, the century of Galileo, Copernicus, Kepler, and Newton. Of course, science had its roots in the past, but it was in this century that we have the beginning of the scientific revolution which culminates in the Newtonian image of nature.

It may sound strange that the development of physics should have any bearing on morality. One might ask, What has physics to do with morality? What difference does it make to ideas of right and wrong whether the sun goes around the earth, or the earth goes around the sun? If the relation of physics to morality is stated in this way the scientific revolution seems to have no bearing on morality. But such an account is superficial. The deeper conflicts between physics and the traditional views of morality were not on the surface. The real trouble started when many came to the conclusion that within the Newtonian image of nature—nature as ruled by strict mechanical laws—there was no place for the religious belief in the moral order of the world. For the Middle Ages the world was at the center of the universe, privileged in its position, the destined abode of the children of God. For the new science the world was a small sphere in the midst of an infinite number of spheres. This new image of the world was devoid of any purpose, and was in no need of a designer. In such a world there was no place for a cosmic moral order. Thus, for many morality became an episodic affair, a merely human creation on a planet that was in time to become uninhabitable.

Another trend that favored moral relativism was the Darwinian theory of the emergence of man. From the Darwinian evolutionary point of view man is the result of natural processes and an integral part of the animal world. His activities — individual, family, social, moral, religious—must be explained in terms of the struggle for survival. Nature is prodigal of life, and there is no room for every being that might be born. Each individual and each group seeks to maintain itself in conflict with the others. In this competition some have advantageous variations, and others have disadvantageous ones. The key concepts of evolutionary morality are adaptation, the struggle for existence, and the survival of the fittest. The strong survive, the weak are destroyed. That was and is the way of nature. In such a setting the traditional moral ideas of justice or equality had no meaning.

Still another trend that helped moral relativism was the intense study of different cultures by the anthropologists. From the anthropological point of view, a view which flowered in the latter part of the nineteenth century, morality came to mean the mores or customs of different cultures. Different cultures had different mores and thus had different morals. One moral system was not better than another; they were simply different. Good and bad, right and wrong had to be interpreted in terms of the customs of the group. Sumner, one of the pioneers of this view, argues that mores can make anything right. Westermarck, a leading moral relativist, similarly justifies the existence of every kind of custom, especially those having to do with marriage. Many Mohammedans believe in and practice polygamy; many Tibetans believe in and practice polyandry; Eskimos have the custom of lending their wives to guests. A study of such customs tends to make one skeptical of the superiority of any one marriage custom. For the anthropologist there are no absolute moral standards but different patterns of life that are equally valid.

The recent trends in psychology strengthened the relativistic view of morality. Freud opened our eyes to new layers of human nature and showed the far-reaching consequence of sex drives. He disturbed the whole puritanic tradition by exhibiting the mental damages that result from suppressed wishes. The aim of life should not be the moralistic repression of natural instincts, but the conscious release of every particle of human energy. As a matter of fact, for Freud most of our actions are controlled below the threshold of consciousness. The role of reason seems to be to ratify such actions by way of "rationalization." And also behaviorism, especially of the Watsonian type, gave a blow to the absolutistic type of morality. For the behaviorist there is only body and behavior; more precisely, stimulus and response. The key concept for complex behavior is conditioned response. Human beings form their habits or character by being exposed to different stimuli in their environment. This process of human conditioning is similar in principle to the conditioning of rats, guinea pigs, dogs, and cats to new types of behavior in the psychologist's laboratory. Thus, in this view moral activities are to be explained not by inherent moral principles but by the adaptive conditioning through indoctrination.

The most recent relativistic theory is based on the semantic studies of ethical terms, such as good and bad, right and wrong. Logical positivists like R. Carnap and A. J. Ayer and philosophers like Charles L. Stevenson argue that statements with meaning must be either of the logical variety which can be analytically established or of the factual variety which can be empirically verified. Ethical terms, it is claimed, are neither of these; they are pseudo-concepts, merely emotive expressions. "You acted wrongly in stealing" simply conveys the notion that you stole money with the additional emotive disapproval. From this point of view ethical terms merely express the feeling of the actor or his wish that others should feel like himself. In such a view of morality absolutistic laws have no place.

So far some of the major scientific trends that have brought about the dominance of relativistic morality have been indicated; but to account fully for this kind of morality it is also necessary to examine the great social, political, and economic changes we have passed through in our industrial, technological, and atomic era. Since everything in our world is changing, it is believed that morals have to change too.

II

The traditional absolutistic moralities are no longer tenable; they belong to the past, to the prescientific eras. The subtler absolutistic moralities mainly offered by the idealistic philosophers are also difficult to entertain. It is impossible to regain the absolute certainty that characterized the absolute moral standards of the past. Yet present-day morality demands some common, universal standards. Is it possible to have such standards or principles on the basis of the modern outlook?

The relativists are correct in their assertions that there is no evidence for any cosmic moral order, that morality is a purely human enterprise. They are also correct in showing that different groups and different cultures have different moral systems.

But the relativists are not convincing in their arguments that we cannot have a common, universal morality. It may be that the basic principles of morality are relative not to particular cultures or periods but to human nature as such. If this is true it should be possible to formulate some relatively universal moral standards. It is this qualified relativity that will now be argued for and that will resolve the modern dilemma of morality if the reasoning is tenable as is being hoped.

But before the possibility of universal standards can be argued about, the meaning and function of morality must be made clear.

Historically, morality has had two different functions in human conduct. One of these was to place restraints on human instincts and desires. Being moral has frequently meant what we should not do. But this negative attitude towards conduct offends our more virile nature. Most of us at some time must have hated the demands of morality in restraining some of our dearest wishes. Another and a more positive function of morality has been the attempt to discover and to realize the patterns of conduct that would make life as satisfactory as possible. I am adopting this second function of morality for my discussion. In this positive sense the task of morality resolves itself into a single question. What is the nature of human good? This can be empirically determined because it is inherent in human experience. As against groping more or less blindly for the conditions that would make for a satisfying life, morality represents an intelligent attempt to discover these conditions, that is, to get away from the hit-or-miss groping. The function of morality is to survey the situation of life as a whole and to formulate such ends as provide the most satisfactory plan for life. As a recent ethicist suggests, the task of morality may be defined as "an attempt to be forehanded and foresighted on a large scale, and to lay down, ahead of the immediate needs of conduct, the lines along which successful living is likely to run."[1]

To state the nature of morality more precisely two interre-

---

[1] Rogers, A. K., *The Theory of Ethics*, New York, Macmillan, 1922, p. 2.

lated concepts should be clarified: the concept of good or value, and the concept of moral good or moral value.

By way of introduction to the analysis of the notion of good or value a few examples should be cited. A pen is good when it writes well, a watch is good when it indicates time correctly, a wine is good when it satisfies our taste, a musical performance is good when it gives us aesthetic joy, and it is good to have a friend. We also say that he is a good man and that the decision of the judge is good and just. Such examples could be multiplied indefinitely.

In the above examples there are three different meanings of good. The first two instances, those of the pen and the watch, convey the meaning of good as being useful for a specific purpose. The next three instances, those of the wine, the music performance, and a friend, are difficult to reduce to the status of means to an end. They represent experiences that are good in themselves and need no further justification, that is, need not be considered as means to some end. One might say, of course, that wine is good for one's digestion, and music for one's nerves, and a friend for one's psychic health, but what is an end may also be a means in some other relation, these values are intrinsic in their usual contexts. The final two instances, those of the good man and of the good decision of the judge are usually referred to as moral values. Our present concern is with the second type of instance, or with intrinsic good.

How may one interpret the nature of intrinsic good or value?

According to one view it is an immediate intuition. Value is said to be the immediate quality of certain objects, and this quality is taken to be ultimate and indefinable. We can only say that "value is value," or "goodness is goodness." One of the strong defenders of this view was G. E. Moore. His view of value has often been discussed and found to be unsatisfactory. Without going into the complex problem of definition one can understand what is meant by an indefinable quality. Usually sense qualities are taken to be such. In trying to give the meaning of yellowness, for example, I may finally say "yellow is yellow." Goodness for

Moore is supposed to be analogous to a sense quality. But there is no qualitative content to "goodness" that is in any way analogous to an original sense impression.

Another view of value, and one that is akin to Moore's is that of N. Hartmann. For Hartmann values are pure essences possessing self-existent being; ". . . values subsist independently of the consciousness of them. Consciousness can grasp or miss them, but cannot make them or spontaneously decree them."[2] Although cognition of values takes place in experience, they present a new dimension of experience not explicable in terms of natural events. Hartmann as the defender of this conception of value is primarily a metaphysical logician. Yet value experience, whatever may be said of it, is a form of human experience. A psychological, empirical account of value seems to be much more fruitful and convincing.

Still another alternative view of value is that it is a distinctive attitude which we adopt toward an object or situation. Usually this notion means that the goodness of anything consists in its being an object of desire. Other terms that can stand for desire would be "wish," "interest," "drive," "propensity," "determining tendency." As a preliminary definition of value one may say that value stands for an object of any desire. The desire may be to get some food, to listen to music, to obtain a position, to accumulate wealth, to win someone's heart, or to worship God. R. B. Perry has given one of the most persuasive accounts of value in terms of interest. Value, for him, "attaches promiscuously to all objects of all interest,"[3] and interest stands for "motor-affective activity."

I agree with Perry's approach to the notion of value but for one modification. Though I take desire or interest to be the source of value, the definition of value as the object of desire is incomplete. It is true that there are no values independent of desire, yet this description falls short of the fact that goodness, or value, is primarily a judgment, an act of reflective recognition. Value, therefore, I take to be approval of the object of desire. In more activistic terms value is the approval of the fulfillment of

---

[2] *Ethics,* trans. by Hauton Coit, New York, Macmillan, 1930, Vol. I, p. 218.

a desire. The distinction I am making is akin to Dewey's distinction in the realm of knowledge, between having an experience and knowing an experience. In the realm of value one must distinguish between having and approving the fulfillment of a desire.

Approval in the present context has no moral implication. First of all, approval, like sense perception, has objective reference; it is the awareness that so and so is good. Secondly, approval in its generic sense means that the fulfillment of desire brings satisfaction. Thus, one may define value as whatever on reflection gives the feeling of satisfaction. The satisfaction through approval is, of course, the result of the satisfaction one gets in the fulfillment, but approval adds something to the fulfillment—a judgment of value.[4]

Though this view of value has some affinity to hedonism, strictly it is not hedonism. For in this definition of value one is not taking pleasure or satisfaction as the motive of action; the motive of action is the dynamic tendency of desire. Very seldom one takes pleasure as the explicit aim of action. Pleasure is not the ultimate of biological activity; it is functionally related to that activity. The definition of value in terms of approval is not concerned with the motive for action, but with the test by which an object or objective is determined to be good or bad.

One more point. If approval springs from a feeling of satisfaction how can it be a judgment? The analysis of a simple judgment of sense preception may help to make this clear. When one says, "This wine is sweet," he assumes that the sweet taste is in himself; yet one has the tendency to assume that the sweetness is present in the wine. One transfers to the object the quality one experiences; in addition to having the sweet sensation one judges the wine as being sweet. In approval the situation is similar. Approval is a satisfying experience, but it is also a judgment. Something one experiences—satisfactoriness— is transferred to the object on which one reflects. Just as "sweetness" is

---

[3] *General Theory of Value,* New York, Longman, Green & Company, 1936, p. 28.
[4] I follow here A. K. Roger's discussion of value. See *The Theory of Ethics,* New York, Macmillan, 1922, Chapters I-III.

attributed to wine, so satisfactoriness is attributed to the object of approval.

So far I have been discussing the theory of value without any reference to moral value. Usually in the discussion of moral value the word "ought" is introduced. Before proceeding to analyze the nature of the moral ought it will be convenient to refer to Kant's theory of ought. For Kant moral good is objectively valid, and the ought is categorically and unconditionally necessary. He regards oughtness as not only a constituent part of moral experience but as the whole of moral experience. Not the good, but duty is for him the ultimate moral concept. The thesis of the present discussion is that the ultimate definition of morality has to be in terms of the notion of the good, or of the satisfactory life, and that duty is only one aspect of the moral situation.

Since my approach is empirical and naturalistic, I should make the basic premise of morality clearer. The central aim of morality is not so much the performance of duty but, more positively, the discovery and realization of the most satisfactory way of life. In this endeavor morality attempts to harmonize conflicting desires and demands. Morality looks to the human good, to the good as a whole, to the good that is permanent, to the good in the light of ideal possibilities. This is the major premise of morality.

This pursuit demands reflection and discrimination, and introduces the notion of the "better." There are situations where the fulfillment of my desire, though good in itself, may harm others. Here there is a conflict between desires. The problem is not what is good, but what is "better," the better being what gives deeper satisfaction.

The context of moral activity consists of human desires and the conflict between them. The aim of morality is not merely the satisfaction of simple, isolated desires. Some desires express primitive appetites, while others express wider, social interests; some give momentary pleasure, while others give deeper satisfaction; some conflict with other desires, while others are harmonious. The aim of morality is to select the better, or to enlighten and harmonize desires so that life may flourish.

It should also be pointed out that the aim of morality is not only to organize one's own desires, but the desires of individuals as members of a society, and also the desires of social groups in relation to other social groups. The social aim of morality is thus to maintain a harmonious way of life for all individuals and ultimately for all social groups. It is from the nature of this aim that the notion of the moral "ought" emerges. But it should always be emphasized that the primary concern of morality is the human good. The "ought" is not a categorical imperative as Kant argued, but hypothetical and conditional; it is not a moral ultimate, but is to be vindicated by good consequences.

The moral "ought," though a derived concept, has its important function in the moral pursuit.

The moral "ought" in its early stages is primarily a restraining force exerted upon impulse or desire. As such a force it is a bare "ought not" which carries no necessary reference in consciousness to an alternative "better." A. K. Rogers, who develops this phase of "ought" in detail, says, "For the peculiarity of the sense of oughtness I am able to discover no underlying reason except this new fact that there is aroused in me a feeling of repugnance and dislike."[5] This emotional repugnance restrains some of our desires, and leaves us uneasy when we disregard it.

At some stage the "ought not" is changed to "ought" and the performance of moral action becomes desirable. Take as illustration the sense of justice. To our intense desire for self-gratification are opposed the demands of others. Justice is primarily concerned with the reconciliation of these conflicting demands. Various considerations may gradually help to attain this end. The feeling of fair play may have a certain degree of restraining influence. Though such a motive is not by itself sufficiently strong, it is a factor for those who wish to keep their integrity. The feeling of sympathy, emphasized by Buddhism, is another factor that helps toward the reconciliation of conflicting demands. In sympathy we put ourselves into the situation of another and feel his suffering and his assertive claim. These two factors are not usually sufficient to reconcile the self-interest of the individual with the

---

5 *Ibid.*, p. 78.

demands of others. But we may gradually come to realize that mutual agreement is preferable to our self-exploitation, that human interests are not as inconsistent as we usually believe them to be, that through cooperative activity we may achieve our own interests more fully. There is also the feeling of exaltation in activities that involve larger human interests. Justice thus becomes an ideal worth pursuing. In the end, paradoxically, there may be nothing which I so much want to do as what I ought to do. The opposition is not between "ought" and desire, but between one desire and another desire.

III

We come now to the central issue. Is it possible to have moral standards within the qualified relativistic outlook of morality that has just been described?

First, as to the meaning of moral standards. By standards are not meant commands or rules to be obeyed categorically without reference to reason. Nor are standards mere generalizations or results of intuition or abstract reasoning. They are judgments of approval of what we should or should not desire. And these judgments have also a vital connection with human action since they function as guides to what we ought to do. Can it be said, then, that moral standards actually exist?

If "goodness" or "ought" is rooted in desires and feelings, the objection usually made is that such a view fails to justify the objectivity of moral standards and ideals. As H. Rashdhall says, ". . . if goodness of an act means simply that the act occasions a specific emotion in particular men, then the same act may be at one and the same time good and bad. Moral feelings will have no more objective truth or validity than any other feelings which vary in their nature or intensity with the varying sensibility of different men's skins or sensory nerves."[6] I have not been arguing that moral values and standards are to be reduced to mere immediate feelings, but rather that a certain type of action elicits in me a feeling of approval and its opposite a feeling of dis-

[6] *Theory of Good and Evil*, Second Edition, Oxford University Press, Vol. I, pp. 145-6, 1924.

approval. And yet it is true that feelings of approval change and with them our judgments of what is good and what is bad, and it is also true that different individuals may have different feelings of approval. There is thus nothing in feeling which gives infallibility to moral standards. But if we face the moral situation on purely intellectual grounds, we are confronted by the same difficulty. As was said of feelings, ideas too change, and different individuals can have different ideas, so that there is no *a priori* ground on which to settle the conflict of standards.

But because moral standards are rooted in feelings and desires, and have no cosmic lodgement outside of human experience, and because to a degree they are variable, it does not follow that we cannot distinguish between the purely arbitrary and the valid forms of standards.

The possibility of universal standards depends upon whether generic human needs exist, since it is such needs that the type of morality which is here being suggested would have to aim at satisfying. That such generic needs exist happens to be true. Human desires and aspirations over a large and most significant area are the same. There will, of course, always be some who deviate from what is common to society as a whole. There are abnormal aggressors, hardened criminals, confused psychopaths, and amoral geniuses. However, the notion of normality does not preclude degrees of variation. Yet by and large what one wants is what other human beings want.

The major human needs and aspirations—survival, health, comfort, ambition, love, happiness—are everywhere essentially the same. Of course they may vary under different conditions. In a primitive society ambition is satisfied by hunting, in a pastoral society by raising cattle, in the modern capitalistic society by accumulating wealth. Even such a custom as human sacrifice in primitive societies becomes meaningful on careful examination. If we, too, believed that sacrificing human beings to evil powers was necessary to the safety of our society, we most probably would act in more or less the same way. Yet different societies do not differ in their basic values. They differ primarily in their knowledge of the nature of the world they live in. It is also true that in time desires may acquire new and deeper meanings, but such possibilities are not peculiar to any one society.

If there is justification for asserting that human beings have common needs and aspirations, then it is possible to formulate universal standards of morality. The source of these standards is not extra-human, for it is none other than the human constitution itself with its apparatus of desires. The function of the standards is to so organize desires that the maximum good will result.

By way of illustration a few historic moral standards or ideals will be indicated that may be regarded as more or less universal. The three slogans of the French Revolution—liberty, equality, and fraternity—are significant moral ideals of this kind.

Though the meaning of liberty has changed from time to time it has been a universal aspiration of human beings. Liberty recognizes the individual's need to make his own decisions and choices. It embraces the whole of his self-expression—the right to think for himself, to pursue his ambition, to marry according to his choice, to follow the religion he prefers. There is a negative liberty and a positive liberty; the one refers to the removal of obstacles to the fulfillment of wishes, and the other to the establishment of the conditions that are necessary for full self-development. The moral ideal of liberty in a society requires the maximum freedom of each individual that is consistent with the same right for all others. This ideal has its roots in human needs and aspirations.

Equality, like liberty, has been a universal aspiration. Equality means justice in society. It recognizes the feeling that "I am as good as you are." But to make sense of this standard one must regard it as prescriptive rather than descriptive. The idea of equality does not deny the obvious fact of unequal natural endowments. Equality demands that all individuals must be given equal opportunity to develop themselves. Fixed inequalities perpetuate injustice. It should be noted that in the kind of world we live in, equality is not granted unless one demands it and is willing to fight for it.

As for fraternity, many religions have preached it, many

ethical systems have argued for it, many political movements have fought for it. Fraternity goes beyond the idea of equality. Fraternity not only implies respect for the rights of others, but asserts kinship with them. In fraternity my fellow-beings are not merely other beings, but my other self. To the growth of this identification there is no limit. This identification may embrace not only my friends and fellow citizens, but alien races and the whole of humanity.

Still another central moral ideal is the ideal of the cooperative society. This ideal calls for "a world, inhabited by many wills, in which each will pursuing its utmost desire shall in so doing serve to the utmost each other doing the same."[7]

These standards or ideals are universal not in the sense that every individual or every group has adhered to them, but in the sense that in human history they have been the major aspirations and fruitful guiding principles. The primary human effort has to be to increase the area of common agreement on these and similar ideals. As A. Edel says, "Ethics could . . . be defined as the effort of men who have some basic agreements to widen the area of common agreement."[8]

Yet these moral standards have no power or authority unless we individually feel their lure. Whoever does not know the excitement of authentic choices and decisions cannot have allegiance to liberty; whoever does not have the sense of fairness in human relations cannot be equalitarian; whoever does not experience the joy of loving and being loved cannot be devoted to the ideal of fraternity. Unless one feels these values, it is futile to argue for them.

IV

The necessity of moral standards and principles has been argued and the possibility of such standards has been indicated. There are a few other issues connected with moral standards that should be stated.

First, it should be noted that the pursuit of moral ideals presents certain difficulties. Human beings have primitive drives,

---

[7] Singer, E., *On Contented Life*, New York, Henry Holt & Co., 1923, p. 84.
[8] *Ethical Judgment*, Glencoe, Ill., The Free Press, 1955, p. 89.

potent ambitions which when fulfilled defeat the pursuit of others. The extreme expression of this spirit is in the Nietzschean "man of might" whose desire is not to attain power but to over-power others. The same spirit, though on a smaller scale, drives many to subordinate others to their own ambition. And this attitude attains greater force and violence when groups get into conflict. R. Niebuhr and other social philosophers remind us that in group relations "power must be challenged by power," that the power of self-interest and egoism is dominant in all inter-group relations. Political and economic groups as they increase in size tend to become impersonal and a law unto themselves. Finally, many of our cultural inheritances which have become our way of living are great hindrances to moral activity. Many of our ways of life—political, economic, and national—have been formed under pressures of conflict and violence. We cannot easily emancipate ourselves from the cultural habits of the past. This fact will not be less true in the future. Although future man may emancipate himself from the hindrances of our past, he may acquire others. This tendency makes the attainment of moral ideals difficult and the moral task an endless one.

Secondly, moral standards have to be exposed from time to time to critical examination, to pragmatic tests. Moral standards are not unalterable absolutes. Their purpose is human happi-ness. As we learn more about the world and our nature, we have to modify our moral standards. Moral standards are in many respects akin to scientific hypotheses; they may be put to the test to determine their desirability, which is to be found in their consequences.

During the last fifty years we have modified our sex stand-ards. Because of new psychiatric knowledge and the growth of secularism and the occurrence of two world wars the changes had to come. Many of the changes have been desirable, but some have been disturbing. Great changes have also occurred in the relation between capital and labor. Higher wages, more collective bar-gaining, and greater security for the workers have been the issues. Here, again, we are groping towards new moral standards. What is most urgent at the moment is the need of formulating standards to regulate the relation between nations and between races. Most of our attitudes in this area are still primitive, though because of atomic weapons our very survival depends on the standards we set up. The final test for all of these changes is pragmatic; the consequences must be beneficial to human beings.

Finally, we have to develop more understanding and tolerance when considering moral standards. We can hardly claim that we have the final answers to many disturbing moral issues. Once we leave the practical, everyday level of moral judgment we are involved in many complex problems. In final analysis our moral standards involve acts of faith. We must assume that there is a generic human nature, that there are common human needs and aspirations. And we must also assume—and this is an even greater assumption—that we can determine exactly what constitutes the common nature.

In the interest of sanity we should try from time to time to view human life dispassionately. Not unlike creative artists, we should try to identify ourselves with a large variety of human beings. Such an approach to the human scene will make us realize that it takes all sorts of people to make a world. We shall find that some rejected drifters have more meaning in their lives than some successful executives of great concerns. Some unmarried couples may have a finer spiritual relationship than some couples whose marriage was sanctioned by the church. Our opponents may have traits that we ought to appreciate and even emulate. We may find some worthwhile values in the eastern societies, and the eastern societies may find some worthwhile values in ours. We seldom add to the cause of moral growth by pretending to be better than our neighbors or by making censoriousness a virtue. This does not mean that we must tolerate the intolerable or that we must be too indulgent toward what we think is wrong. Tolerance need not weaken our practical moral commitments. It saves us from pomposity and from the illusion that only one form of good is worthwhile. Somehow we have to combine genuine tolerance with vigorous commitments.

This general approach to the modern dilemma of morality has been a naturalistic one. It has been asserted that no act can be regarded as moral or immoral without reference to its consequences as these affect our desires. Far from denying the importance of moral standards, the naturalistic approach recognizes them as essential to human happiness, and only maintains that they must be empirically determined.

Chapter VII

THE FUNCTION OF ART

A rt is a universal aspect of human life; there is no activity—
scientific, religious, moral, economic, or political—that
may not give rise to aesthetic expression. Art raises many
questions: What is the nature of art? What are the modes of
art? What are the sources of art? What is the relation of art
to other human activities, The primary concern here will be
with the function of art in human life. But first a few remarks
should be made on the nature of art.

I

The attempt to understand the nature of art faces an initial
difficulty. The experience of art might seem to defy analysis;
"ineffable" may occur to us as the only word not incongruous
with the aesthetic experience, and yet one cannot abandon
analysis. The first impact of a work of art may be "ineffable,"
but at a later moment the desire to understand our experience
demands analysis.

In dealing with art certain preliminary distinctions have
to be made. Art as a general term is used for any object made
for any purpose whatsoever. There are different modes of art
and though these modes are interrelated they have different
functions. Time-pieces, sewing machines, and cars are works
of art; so are paintings, sculptures, and symphonies. The former,
or the technical arts, are only the means for purposes external
to them; their function is usefulness. Time-pieces are made to
indicate time, sewing machines to sew, cars to transport. As
useful arts they are replaceable by new developments, they have
no intrinsic value. The latter, or the fine arts, are symbols of
value and so embody intrinsic meanings. In painting, sculpture,
music, or any other of the fine arts the meanings in the products

are not merely referential, but have a unique value and are irreplaceable.

Sometimes these two modes of art are closely interrelated. A dagger may be a useful weapon for defense as well as a beautiful object; a painting may be an effective description of an historic situation as well as an object of aesthetic pleasure. In the present discussion the term "art" will be limited to the fine arts unless the adjective "technical" is added.

What then is art? The answer to this question is elusive and difficult. After many centuries of discussion the question is not yet fully answered. One of the oldest answers is that art is essentially imitation. Plato and after him Aristotle gave expression to this theory. Yet this answer is too simple to be satisfactory. If art is merely an imitation of the original, why, as Socrates points out, should we go to art? Is not the original superior? Another theory of art of long tradition is the claim that the aesthetic experience is an insight into some transcendent reality. For Plato, and later for many Platonists, beauty belongs to the realm of Ideas or Forms, and these are perfect, absolute, immutable. A given beautiful object partially expresses and vaguely reminds one of the absolute beauty. Coming to the modern era, the answers to the question about the nature of art are more empirical and analytic. Thinkers like Schiller, Spencer, and Groos suggested the play-theory of art. They claimed that the play theory with its emphasis on biological origins, activity and function made aesthetic experience more intelligible and vital. Many other aestheticians made the conative and affective aspect of human response more crucial to art. Common to these theories is the assertion that art or the aesthetic experience is an expression or objectification of human feeling and desires. For Tolstoy art is the 'language of emotion'; for Santayana it is 'objectified pleasure'; for Parker it is the imaginative expression of a wish. There are still other theories. For the idealist Croce art is the 'intuition' or 'expression' of color-images, line-images, word-images which are meaningful and charged with feeling. For Clive Bell, who has been a champion of the new developments in art, art is 'significant form' divorced from objects of ordinary experience.

These and many other contemporary theories of art are full of insight into the nature of art; there are also complementary theories on the complex structure of art, yet no one theory seems to have attained finality. Nor does the present discussion make such a claim. What the present discussion is concerned with is the presentation of a tentative description of the nature and function of art to make clearer the role of art as an ideal in human life.

Art is a form of language and thus presents a triadic relation. The artist or the creator has something to say, the painting, poem, or musical piece is what is being said; and the spectator, reader, or listener is the one who is being addressed. The artist himself may also be the spectator. As Matisse is reported to have said, "When a painting is finished, it is like a new-born child. The artist, himself, must have time for understanding it." There will be occasion to refer to all three aspects of art, which are closely related. The experience of the spectator, whether he be the artist or another observer, will be considered first.

The spectator comes to his experience of art with two basic predispositions—the biological and the cultural. The capacity for the biological response, whether reflexive, instinctive, or emotional is transmitted from generation to generation and carries no acquired characteristics. The capacity for the cultural responses, whether attitudes, beliefs, or ideas, is based on traditions, cultures, or customs, and is thus transmitted from parent to offspring and carries only acquired characteristics. Although these two types of predisposition are different, they are both significant and vitally interrelated.

The response to an art object is not a single emotion, like joy, anger, or fear. A single emotion in isolation is a weakening one and lacks significance. If an art object elicits only a single emotion one could then agree with Plato that art "feeds and waters the passions instead of drying them up; lets them rule, although they ought to be controlled, if mankind is ever to be increased in happiness and virtue." The artist always evokes more than one emotion. As Cassirer says, "What we feel in art

is not a simple or single emotional quality. It is the dynamic
process of life itself—the continuous oscillation between opposite
poles, between joy and grief, hope and fear, exultation and
despair. To give aesthetic form to our passions is to transform
them into a free active state. In the work of the artist the
power of passion itself has been made a formative power."[1] In
music, poetry, or drama, where the stimuli are presented in
sequence one is moved from one emotion to another. In those
forms of art where stimuli are presented simultaneously, as in
painting, sculpture, and architecture, one still moves from one
part to another, and, as the artist intends, from one emotion to
another.

The artist, by the fusion of varied emotions, images, and
ideas creates a mood, or in the Deweyian sense an "experience."
The mood is characterized by unity, a unity that involves discrete
states of response but is not reducible to isolated parts. The
mood has also temporal endurance, and what endures is not so
much what is perceived or conceived but what is emotionally
experienced. We speak of the joyful or melancholy mood and
of the exalted or depressed mood. What, then, is the nature of
the aesthetic mood?

The first thing to observe is that the aesthetic mood is a
state of agitation or tension. In observing a painting, or listen-
ing to music, or reading a poem emotions are awakened, and
the deeper the emotion the more disturbing is the response. The
artist arouses in us a sense of values and the sense of revaluation.
Art, as Singer observes, "moves us *out of ourselves.*"[2] And to be
thus "transformed" can mean nothing more than "*to be changed
as to one's purpose*; it is to enter on a world in which things
are revalued." The artist is a "messenger of discontent;" he
detaches us from our old estimate of values to "*self-abandon-
ment.*"[3]

Yet this state of activity is contemplative. The very essence
of the aesthetic mood is an active passivity, a kind of thoughtful
tension. In aesthetic experience contemplation is apprehension,

[1] *An Essay on Man,* New York, Doubleday, 1952, p. 190.
[2] *On Contented Life,* New York, Henry Holt & Co., 1936, p. 31.
[3] *Ibid.,* p. 32.

one is not primarily interested in the truth or proof of what is apprehended or in its practical consequences but in the apprehension as a value in itself.

And although the artist inspires contemplative agitation, he advocates no new ideal to be fulfilled. The artist is not a teacher giving us new knowledge; nor is he a moralist suggesting new guides toward the good life; nor is he a preacher forcing the sinner into repentance. What the artist does is to arouse in us the experience of a value. As Singer says, the artist "creates the creator" of ideals. At his best he gives us a sense of rich fulfillment or exaltation. It must be added that the specific evocations of art are varied. Some works of art amuse us, others charm us, and still others stir us. Yet taken collectively art may be said to contribute to the renewal of the human spirit, to the sense of courage.

The focus so far has been on the nature of the aesthetic mood. There is, of course, the structural aspect of art, which the artist must manipulate as effectively as possible, but this aspect will not be given here.

II

The analysis of the nature of art leads to the question of the function of art in human life. The most pervasive function of art, art taken collectively and at its best, is the renewal of the human spirit, a renewal akin to the mystic's experience, but this renewal has a variety of dimensions.

First, art brings satisfaction and joy through an imaginative world. The spectator participates in new vistas or new possibilities, such as are not open to him on his everyday life. Potentialities and repressed desires can hardly be fulfilled through this means. As DeWitt Parker points out, "there are two ways in which wishes can find satisfaction—the real way and the dream way."[4] In the real way one deals aggressively with one's immediate environment to achieve satisfaction, but in the dream way one's desires are fulfilled only in a world of fantasy. For any real satisfaction of a desire there is also possible an imaginary

---

4 *The Analysis of Art,* Yale U Pre, 1926, pp. 3-4.

satisfaction, but there are certain desires, as for instance the acquisition of great wealth, which usually can only be satisfied through the imagination.

There are several characteristics of dreams. There is, first of all, an 'as if' attitude in dream fulfillment. What we dream, especially what we day-dream, is taken to be 'as if' real. For the time being the food we produce, the wealth we accumulate, the position we attain are actual. But, also, there is always a fringe of day-dreaming that we take to be unreal. In this make-believe one part of us believes, another part disbelieves; it is the combination of belief and disbelief which constitutes the 'as if' attitude.

Aesthetic experience like dreams and day-dreams gives imaginary satisfaction. In observing Giorgione's *Concert Champêtre* one lives for a time in an idyllic setting; in reading a novel like Tolstoy's *War and Peace* one participates in great human dreams and achievements; in watching *Bacchante* by Frederick W. MacMonnies one enjoys the experience of frenzy. The same is true enough, in a somewhat different way, in music and architecture. Music creates new moods and aspirations and satisfies many unexpressed and subconscious desires; magnificent temples lift our spirits and give grandeur to life. Art in all its forms is a source of imaginative satisfaction. Yet art does more than fulfill unsatisfied desires, it also gives expression to superabundant joys. The notion that art is always an escape from pain does only partial justice to the aesthetic experience. There is the art of the triumphant mood. As Parker says, "The theory that art is the expression of painful lives is incapable of explaining such ebullitions as a festive song, a triumphal arch, or the hundreds of pictures painted by men of large and happy lives and abounding health, like Titian and Renoir. It cannot explain the art of joy, a Monet landscape, or Whitman's 'Sound my barbaric yawp over the roofs of the world.' "[5]

Though art gives imaginary satisfaction to desires it differs in one important respect from dreams and daydreams. In art the dream attains objectivity. Some aestheticians do not consider the objectification in art as important. Croce, for example, de-

---

[5] *Ibid.*, p. 171.

fines art as "intuition" or "expression" which involves all that is concrete and immediate in experience—sense-data, memory, imagination, feeling apart from the actual creative work of art, such as a painting, a statue, or a poem. The latter are mere copies of what the artist has experienced. Yet this neglect of the physical aspect of art is not tenable. Not only is the origin of art in craft, though it goes beyond it, but the creative imagination of the artist and the material he uses for objectification are vitally interrelated; the material both initiates and extends the creativity of the artist. As Bosanquet says, " . . . imaginative expression creates the feeling in creating its embodiment, and the feeling so created not merely cannot be otherwise expressed, but cannot otherwise exist, than in and through the embodiment which imagination has found for it."[6]

Art is also the most effective instrument for civilizing the individual and thus a major source of values. As memory unites our past and present so the artistic creations of the past and present unite to increase our value sense in depth and breadth. Through art the values of civilization become part of us.

What better way to know the values of the Greeks than through Homer, Plato, Aeschylus, and Sophocles and through the Greek temples and sculptures. And the medieval civilization is most effectively experienced through its religious rites, rituals, paintings, cathedrals, sculptures, and songs. And the revolutionary movements and new emerging values of the Renaissance are equally arrived at through the changes that were introduced in architecture, sculpture, painting, poetry, and other forms of imaginative literature.

Through art we participate not only in the values of our culture but in those of other cultures as well. The arts of the South Sea Islands and of the Chinese and of still others have their unique significance in the sphere of values. Through this means we actually bridge the values of the East and West, and of the North and South.

What needs to be emphasized is that through art we can become deeply acquainted with some of the richest values of

---

[6] *Three Lectures on Aesthetics,* London, Macmillan, 1915, p. 34.

the present. In contemporary culture we have not only the values of tradition—those of the Greeks and the Judeo-Christians and the Renaissance—but the new values that are inherent in the extensive development of the sciences and technology and extended global relations. The sciences have brought us nearer to nature, technology has created a new setting, and the extended global relations have expanded the social environment. The new values that have emerged must find expression in contemporary art and thus become part of us.

Art is the most effective means of communicating the best values of the past and present. Although a foreign language may be regarded as something of a barrier to literary communication, not so the foreign paintings, music, and architecture, which as media of communication may be said to constitute the basis of a common humanity.

Finally, art is a source of power, especially in relation to life's painful aspects. Art is not practical in the usual, narrow sense of the word, yet it provides a source of power to meet life in its total impact. Varied forms of art pursue this end.

In the romantic form of art human wishes are satisfied in the world of imagination. Such an experience may be helpful in opening up new possibilities in our development and new vigor in the pursuit of ideals. In satirical art we are exposed to the absurd possibilities of life, yet obliquely in the interest of the corresponding ideals. The satirical exposure of lies, of cruelty in human relations, of hypocrisy in institutional management, and of the idealization of war is really emphasizing the need of honesty and justice and sincerity and the genuine love of peace. Satire is a means of awakening us from a too callous attitude toward life and of promoting a more enlightened attitude. In the realistic or pessimistic form of art our wishes are denied or deflated, and yet it is through this form of art that one can attain the power to face life as it is. If one is to face life with courage and to live at peace with himself he must know all the facts of life—the presence of evil, tragedy, disillusionment, death. Such diverse writers as Leopardi, de Maupassant, and Hardy help us to confront the darker aspects of life.

A major source of courage is in the recollection of past

triumphs over insuperable difficulties. Caesar brings courage to his fear-stricken troops by reminding them of earlier victories: "What, pray, have you to fear? Why do you despair of your own courage or of my competence? We have made trial of this foe in the time of our fathers." Following these words of Caesar, "a marvelous change came over the spirits of all ranks and an utmost ardor for action." Art gives courage in the same manner. The artist by his varied forms and colors, by his movements of sound, or by the conduct of his dramas so plays upon our feelings as to create the mood of courage. In a world where there are radical and irremediable evils and suffering the core of the aesthetic response is bound to be courage.

III

The function of art has often been compared and contrasted with that of morality. Is art compatible with morality or are they ever in conflict?

Art and morality have independent interests. Art is able to flourish in the absence of morality and certain types of artistic creativity may even develop not only apart from morality, but in protest against the common mores. Decadent art, which may have aesthetic value, is often enhanced by decadent life. How then may art and morality live in harmony or continue to exist in unreconciled conflict,

Too often it is assumed that morality is satisfactory and that the only question to be asked is whether art is in harmony with the established moral code. But as John Dewey says, "Imagination is the chief instrument of the good ... the ideal factors in every moral outlook and human loyalty are imaginative. ... Hence it is that art is more moral than moralities."[7] The latter tend to be attached to the *status quo*. As Dewey further argues, the moral prophets of humanity have always been poets even though they spoke in free verse or in parable. Art opens through imagination new possibilities, new ideals in contrast to limited actualities.

And, moreover, by eliciting sympathy and identification

---

[7] *Art As Experience*, New York, Capricorn Books, Putnam, 1954, p. 348.

with a large variety of human beings art fulfills an invaluable function—breadth of understanding. It takes all sorts of people to make a world, and it is the recognition of this truth that frees us from a narrow censoriousness such as is only too frequent in the usual practice of morality. Morality is saturated with the concepts of the good and the bad, of right and wrong, of virtue and vice; it divides human beings into two sharp groups, those it praises and those it admonishes. Sanity demands an occasional orientation that goes beyond good and evil, beyond praise and blame. Art is wholly free of moral obsessions and brings a liberating and uniting spirit to human relations; it understands and appreciates the predicaments of the saints and the sinners, of the respected citizens and the outcasts of society.

Art is also a means of freeing us from our more primitive drives. Man seems to have a dual nature; he is egotistic and aggressive, but he is also sympathetic and cooperative. The primitive aspect is more basic to human nature, whereas the civilized aspect is the result of long discipline under social demands. And yet the primitive self is never fully tamed but insists on reasserting itself. Art provides a medium through which this aspect of human nature may receive imaginative satisfaction. Though Dionysian art is subject to severe condemnation, it does help prevent actual indulgence in disruptive drives by providing an imaginative outlet for them.

And yet like all great human enterprises art may be misused. Art can appeal to good behavior, but it may also make evil seem enticing. And, again, if art is considered as the sole interest in life, so that it gets detached from the urgent, necessary demands of life, it tends to disorganize life. Life is more than art; life is also more than science, more than morality, more than religion; each of these interests has its legitimate place in life. Art is in greater danger of detachment because it is the source of immediate, intrinsic values. There will always be a conflict of interests in human affairs, yet these conflicts have to be resolved in their contexts and with the help of the overall guiding ideal of maximum satisfaction to all human beings.

But despite all the possible abuses of art, the artist must

have full freedom to fulfill his creativity. If art is controlled by political, ideological, commercial, or moral forces this creativity will be maimed. Art can only flourish and grow when it freely pursues its autonomous ideals.

Chapter VIII

THE NEW PERSPECTIVES IN RELIGION

Man is concerned with the fate of what he values most. Yet his power is limited at some point and he needs help to sustain him. It is religion that provides the hope for a source of power that would help him achieve his desire to preserve and promote what he most values. As a recent philosopher says, "... religion is man's *deepest solicitude,* his concern for the fate of that which he accounts most valuable."[1]

What is most valued differs with different men; the thing valued may be personal survival, or group survival, or a cause dear to one's heart, or a great personal ambition, or intense love, or a noble social ideal. The sources of power to promote what is valued differ too. In primitive societies appeals were made to "powers" in their environment; at a later stage appeals were made to unseen spirits, to Mana, to Kami, to the gods of the Greek and Roman Pantheons. And, finally, it was the omnipotent, yet good and righteous God of the Judeo-Christian religion, the God who is concerned with the suffering and destiny of human beings.

I

For many the belief that at the core of reality they have an ally of great power to help them in their struggle has been very valuable. There are, of course, some people, like Ivan Karamazov, who proclaim that there is no god and therefore feel that everything is permissible. Yet for countless individuals a positive belief has been a source of help. For centuries the center of religion has been for many the belief in a personal God and in the immortality of the soul. These beliefs have been dramatized and strengthened by sacred books, dogmas, rituals and rites.

The central beliefs of orthodox religions have been regarded

---

1 Perry, R. B., *Realms of Value,* Cambridge, Harvard U Pre, 1952, p. 463.

as absolute and unalterable. This has been detrimental to the actual growth of religion. As Alfred W. Whitehead wisely remarks, "Religion will not regain its old power until it can face change in the same spirit as does science. Its principles may be eternal, but the expression of these principles requires continual development."[2] The changes in every area of human activity and belief have been so great that despite the resistance of orthodoxy many changes in religion had to come. The function and the status of religious institutions are changing; the religious concepts of man are changing; the traditional concepts of God are changing. The causes of these changes are many and complex. The scientific outlook on the world, the technological developments, and the new economic and political structures have all had their share in these changes. This discussion will be confined to the changes in religious beliefs and ideals as centered in the concepts of God and human destiny.

For the theist, God is a personal, all-powerful being, yet righteous and good. He is the creator of the universe and the guarantor of man's immortality. He is the supreme and ultimate end of man. But whether there is a personal God has to be determined not by what human beings need and wish but by reliable evidence. What is true and what we wish to be true do not always coincide. There is always the tendency, especially in dealing with deeply emotional beliefs, to believe what one wishes to be true. What should be one's theory of evidence to establish beliefs? This question has had a long and thorny history.

The pursuit of knowledge has not been easy. In the early period of the human race many unreliable ways—magic, soothsaying, and astrology—have been the dominant ways of obtaining knowledge. Fear, superstitions, and irrational beliefs have dissipated a great deal of human energy. In everyday situations practical causal relations were observed, but the existent empirical knowledge did not result in fruitful generalizations.

The pursuit of reliable knowledge persisted more responsibly in the historic methods of intuitionism, rationalism, and classic empiricism. These methods offered significant insights, but they

---

[2] *Science and the Modern World,* New York, Pelican, 1948, p. 188.

were limited in scope. Intuition was confined to a private world;
rationalism rightly emphasized the importance of reason, but was
limited to logical systems and so could not give knowledge of the
actual world; classic empiricism, though convincingly asserting the
indispensability of experience for knowledge, unfortunately confined its notion of experience to the immediate, disconnected
succession of sensations.

With the growth of science, a growth that has a long history,
a major breakthrough came about. In the scientific approach to
a given problem hypotheses and theories are suggested which
must be directly or indirectly verifiable. The method is experimental and self-corrective. In the present discussion the method
of science is regarded as the way of knowing facts in every area
of human endeavor. Taking as our guide the modern empirical
or scientific procedure, certain consequences are relevant to religious beliefs. First, as to the facts. The supernaturalistic orientation has been basically undermined by the critical studies of
the sacred books, by the historic accounts of the origin and development of religion, by the astronomical descriptions of the
universe, by the evolutionary doctrine of the origin of life and
the emergence of man, by the recent psychological and psychiatric
studies of human nature, and by the anthropological studies of the
various cultures, traditions, and tribal beliefs. But even more
important than the accumulation of facts that have undermined
supernaturalism is the essential validity of the empirical method
as such. The conflict between science and religion is not always
about specific facts; religious leaders usually attempt to assimilate
new facts into the structure of their dogmas. The real issue is the
way of going about settling questions of fact, and the empirical
method is at the opposite pole from the supernaturalistic approach.

The methods of religion in establishing its beliefs have been
varied. One of the methods has been the division into territories.
St. Thomas Aquinas distinguished "truths of faith" from "truths
of reason." At a later period the distinction was made between
revelation and natural knowledge. The "truths of faith" and
revelation were taken to be independent of the verifiable methods

of science. This view is a disconcerting one. The gap between the two areas need not be permanent; the new developments in knowledge may close the separation more and more. There is no need of drawing far-reaching conclusions from present ignorance.

Another method of religion to establish beliefs has been the mystical one. That there is such a thing as mystical experience need not be denied, but the claim that the mystic is in contact with a transcendental reality may be questioned. What is empirically given in mystical experience are certain human drives in heightened form—mystics often speak of spiritual marriage, of tender embraces—and the values of the society to which the mystic belongs. One may accept the fruits of these experiences—the vision of some supreme good, the spirit of attachment and detachment, and the renewal of spirit without accepting the mystics' highly debatable assumptions. Many have found contentment like that of the mystics in their devotion to ideals that have their basis in human nature and in the culture of their time; and some have found in art a rapture and a renewal like those of the mystics without surrendering an intelligent survey of existence.

There are also many philosophical arguments for the existence of God. Historically the most famous are the cosmological, ontological, and teleological arguments. The cosmological argument tries to prove the existence of God from the idea of a "First Cause"; yet even if such proof were possible, which is very doubtful, it would not prove that such a "First Cause" is worthy of worship. The famous ontological argument of St. Anselm tries to prove the existence of God in a purely logical way by arguing that the idea of perfection implies the existence of God. At present we know that from purely logical premises no existential propositions can be drawn. Historically Kant has already destroyed that argument. The teleological argument comes nearest to presenting empirical evidence. Yet this argument is not convincing, for if there is any evidence for beneficial design, this can be so only for individuals who have already accepted some religious belief.

The most recent defense of religious beliefs has been by way of the religious type of existentialism, especially that of Sören

Kierkegaard, which has had a great vogue among Protestant theologians. Existentialism emphasizes feeling and especially willing. Kierkegaard is basically an irrationalist. Counter to the Hegelian thesis that the real is rational and the rational is real Kierkegaard assumes that the real is irrational and the irrational is real. The Christian faith is not only above reason but contrary to reason. Faith is "against understanding"; it is "divine folly."[3] The proper object of faith is the "absurd"; belief in original sin, in immortality, in God is full of paradoxes. Belief in God, despite its irrationality, is a free, personal decision. Kierkegaard's doctrine is not far from Tertullion's famous saying *"credo quai absurdum."* Similarly for Miguel de Unamuno, who approves Kierkegaard's views, reason and faith are enemies. Faith in immortality is irrational, and belief in God is not rationally tenable; not reason but vital anguish impels us to believe in God. To believe in God is "to long for His existence," and this longing begets faith.[4] If existential thinking would involve one's whole existence, then reason as well as feeling and willing must enter into thinking. But Kierkegaardian existentialism repudiates reason. Not only empirical evidence, but reason itself is rejected. Faith is based on fiat, on arbitrary decision, on the impelling force of anguish. This is, indeed, a desperate way of establishing religious beliefs. Irrational beliefs may be moving forces, but if one knows that his beliefs are irrational he can hardly live with them.

What, then, is the status of religious beliefs, especially of the belief in God? Vast amounts of source material and extensive critical studies have thrown new light on religious phenomena. Historians have given an enlightening account of the birth and growth of religion and of the evolution of the religious dogmas and rites by examining the current economic, political, and cultural conditions. To understand the origin of Christianity one must not only know Judaism and the Gospels but the mysteries

---

[3] *Fear and Trembling*, trans. Robert Payne, London, New York, Oxford University Press, 1939. *passim.*

[4] *The Tragic Sense of Life*, trans., J. E. Crawford Flitch, London, Macmillan, 1926, p. 184.

and the social as well as the political structure of the Roman Empire at that time. And to make sense of the dogmas of the Virgin Mary, the Divinity of Christ, and the Fatherhood of God, one must know the historical and cultural sources of these dogmas. It is thus the historical accounts of religions that have naturalized their supernatural claims. Sociologists through their studies of the relation of society to religion and especially of totemism have shown that religion is rooted in society and that the idea of god is a symbol of the society and its values. Emil Durkheim in examining the elementary characteristics of totemism points out that religion in its simplest form is a collection of beliefs and practices of the group, both sacred and profane, that unify the group into a single moral community. He further maintains that the essential characteristics of all religions are akin to those that constitute totemism. Thus, it is concluded that society is the basis of religion. For Durkheim, "Religious force is only the sentiment inspired by the group in its members, but projected outside of the consciousness that experience them, and objectified,"[5] and the concept of the supreme god is the expression of the sentiment of group unity. The psychologists and psychoanalysts have made intelligible the place of religion in the individual's life by emphasizing the functional nature of religious belief in the crises and struggles of human beings. A common theme expressed by many psychologists is that a man, as one of the functionalists says, "creates whatever concepts and principles he may need in order to make himself master of the phenomena and of his environment. To the same end were the gods created."[6] Similarly from the psychiatric point of view, as Freud argues: "when the child grows up and finds that he is destined to remain a child forever, and that he can never do without protection against unknown and mighty powers, he invests these with the traits of the father-figure; he creates for himself the gods, of whom he is afraid, whom he seeks to propitiate, and to whom he

---

[5] *The Elementary Forms of Religious Life,* trans. by J. W. Swain, New York, Macmillan, p. 229.

[6] Foster, George B., *The Function of Religion,* Chicago, U. Chicago Pr., 1909, p. 84.

nevertheless entrusts the task of protecting him."[7]

God, then, is God-idea, the projection of human ideas and values. Gods are the creations of human wishes. One's god is what one values most—power, security, wealth, knowledge, love. In traditional religions these values are idealized and personified as gods in a supramundane realm. Actually these gods are cultural and poetic symbols. There are symbols of great institutions, symbols of country, symbols of national spirit. Similarly, God as Lord of Hosts, King, Judge, or Father is a cultural symbol having its origin in political, legal, or the more intimate family values. In a more inclusive sense god is the symbolic, mythical expression of the highest aspirations of the human race in a cosmic setting. But by regarding religious beliefs as poetic symbols or myths one need not depreciate them; they carry deep human significance. As George Santayana, a great naturalistic philosopher, says, ". . . religion has the same original relation to life that poetry has; only poetry, which never pretends to literal validity, adds a pure value to existence, the value of a liberal imaginative existence."[8] Whenever Plato failed to give a literal account of great ideas and values he resorted to myths. The *Phaedo* myth, the *Phaedrus* myth of the charioteer, the myth of *Er,* the *Atlantis* myth carry important ideas. Though myths are not true in a literal sense, they express great values and human aspirations. Such are the religious myths.

II

With the passing of the traditional concept of God is there a place for religion? Many believe that if one does not accept the supernaturalistic dogmas one is no longer religious. This attitude is unfortunate, for it limits religion to one of its historic developments, and to one that belongs to older cultures and is rejected by many today. Shall we say that men like Buddha, Spinoza, John Dewey, and Albert Einstein who were among the saintliest of men were not religious because they could not entertain supernaturalistic dogmas? And shall we say that many less

---

[7] *The Future of an Illusion,* Trans. by W. D. Robson-Scott, New York, Liveright Publishing Corp., 1949, p. 42.

[8] *Life of Reason,* New York, Scribner, One Volume Edition, p. 183.

famous people who also reject supernaturalism but who are equally devoted to the highest ideals are not religious? In contrast to the supernaturalistic religion there is the naturalistic religion. And by naturalism we mean that nature is the whole of reality. Nature includes everything we know and might know, and of this knowledge the achievements and aspirations of human beings are an important part.

Religion was earlier described as man's concern to promote and preserve his major values and to help him achieve these values. To what source can we resort to strengthen our efforts and enrich our lives?

First, there is the collective activity of the scientists that will accumulate knowledge with which to help us. But what is especially relevant to the present discussion is that "knowledge is power." God willing and science achieving come to the same result except that the latter is controllable. The belief that through science we can make our way through difficulties is based on the idea that cause discovered is cause controlled. This principle has been the most useful guiding principle in the control of the natural forces.

Secondly, the moral ideal of the cooperative society enriches and strengthens human beings. Science is a great power, but morally it is neutral; it may be used for the benefit of human beings or for their destruction. Especially in our present atomic era we need another source of power to use the power of science and technology for good ends.

Morality is concerned with human desires and with the conflict of desires. The aim of morality is to survey critically these desires and to determine which on the whole are most satisfying. In this pursuit morality tries to harmonize an individual's conflicting personal desires as well as his social ones. It is even more deeply concerned with harmonizing the conflicts between different social groups.

A third source of strength is art. Art at its best, and especially when considered collectively, has a major role in life. Art is a form of language. The artist, the creator, has something to say; what is said is a symbol of thoughtful feeling—a poem, a painting, a musical piece. What the artist says moves us out of ourselves. The deeper the emotion stirred, the more significant is the experience. In this experience one enters a world of new values and a world of new possibilities. The artist arouses in us the creative imagination and in this way provides us with exaltation and courage. If this claim may be made for art, then it is indeed a source of strength. In the human struggle the renewed spirit is of great importance; surely the outcome of man's fight depends to a degree on the spirit with which it is fought.

Although science, morality, and art are independent, they must be pursued together. The power of science needs moral guidance; the activities of science and morality require the invigorating spirit of art. With science, morality, and art we can look forward to unlimited progress. This unity in trinity is the naturalist's religious object of devotion.

For a devoted religious man God is his supreme and ultimate end; for many this is meant to be convertible—a man's ultimate end is his god. The universal and ultimate wish of human beings is the wish to attain the strength to promote and preserve their values. The source of this strength is the united progress of science, morality, and art. It is in the pursuit of this ideal, the ideal to gain more strength, an ideal though not fully attainable, that satisfaction lies. As Singer says, "What god could with better right than . . . Omnipotence calls to man, from out infinity, 'My son, I ought to be thy supreme and ultimate end if thou would be truly blessed?' What life could with better right call itself religious than one spent in lifting its world toward such a god?"[9]

III

Although it has been shown that the joint pursuit of science, morality, and art can be regarded as essentially religious, what remains to be considered is the fact of death. Religion has always been concerned with the final destiny of man. In theism man's immortality is assured. Do we have any evidence for such a belief?

---

[9] *On Contented Life,* New York, Henry Holt & Co., 1936, p. 153.

Man abhors final extinction. All values are rooted in life; naturally human beings facing death hope for an afterlife. In the East a long traditional belief in reincarnation supported both the hope of an afterlife and the demand for final justice. The individual's life was not going to be destroyed since he was to be reincarnated in terms of the kind of life he had lived in his former incarnation. In the West the great story of the resurrection of Jesus Christ after his crucifixion offered the hope of immortality for many. St. Paul's confident faith that death through Jesus is swallowed up in victory has been repeated at innumerable Christian burials. These cultural myths have their poignant value and have comforted their believers. In recent years some apparently empirical attempts have been made to verify an afterlife by communication with the dead. Yet this seeming phenomenon to which the Spiritists appeal may be more reasonably explained by chance, coincidence, and by the subconscious activities of the medium and of whoever else is present. Yet there are certain general considerations supposed to be in favor of immortality that are independent of historic myths and the claim of the Spiritists. Here, again, belief depends on one's theory of evidence.

First, there is the claim that the mind or soul is independent of the body; the disintegration of the body therefore does not imply the disintegration of the mind or soul. The arguments for dualism are many and highly complicated; yet there is no empirical evidence for this view. Mind is the product of natural evolutionary processes. It is the flowering of a complex, organized nervous system. Briefly, mind is the function of body. Any damage to the brain is damage to the mind; complete damage to the brain is complete damage to the mind. There is no brainless mind nor bodiless soul. The biological, physiological, and psychological evidence for the monistic view of body-mind is too strong for such beliefs. Mind or soul, as we know it, is adjectival and not substantive. If we take the cumulative evidence for the dependence of the mind on the body the belief in immortality is hardly defensible. And yet there is a place for the concept of the soul. We speak of an artist's soul, of a saint's soul. And we also refer to the soul of the covetous, the soul of the glutton, the soul of the tyrant. Soul, in an empirical sense, is the expression of the deepest desire of a person, and to the degree that we know a person's deepest desire, to that degree we know his soul.

Secondly, there is the belief, again of long standing, that absolute and spiritual values cannot be destroyed and that since human personalities embody such values they in turn cannot be destroyed. D. C. Macintosh, a distinguished theologian of the recent past, says, " . . . the adequate conservation of spiritual values necessarily involves the conservation of persons. If all genuine spiritual values are to be conserved without final loss, the death of the body cannot mean the end of personal existence."[10] And, again, "If personalities in whom . . . absolute values exist are allowed to sink into nothingness, then faith in the conservation of absolute values is mistaken, and moral optimism is an illusory dream."[11] This claim is doubtful. First, we know nothing whatsoever of absolute values existing independently of human desires. Values are relative to human desires and interests; apart from human desires or those of other sentient beings there are no values. And even if one should think of values as Platonic ideas or universals and thus eternal, as some idealists like N. Hartmann do, such a philosophy of value would have no relevance to immortality. Because a vanishing smoke embodies the universal concept of "smoke" this particular smoke need not be permanent. Lastly, to tie the vital importance of morality to a belief in immortality is an unfortunate doctrine. Morality is a necessity for human good here and now and need not be based on highly doubtful beliefs.

There is one final attempt to support the belief in immortality. The universe, it is claimed, is rational and purposeful; consequently we have the right to believe in the final preservation of the human personality. Many idealists have argued for such a view; but the strongest formulation of this view has been that of the theists. God as the all-powerful, all-good creator of a purposeful world will not, as they affirm, destroy human life.

---

10 *The Reasonableness of Christianity*, New York, Scribner, 1925, p. 65.
11 *Ibid.*, p. 66.

"The world . . . cannot safely be regarded as realizing a *divine* purpose unless man's life continues after death,"[12] says F. H. Tennant, the theologian. He further says, "The righteousness which theism must ascribe to God consists rather in provision of adequate opportunities for the development of all that is potential in God-given personality, conservation of the valuable, and love, such as precludes the mockery of scheming that a rational creature's guiding light through life shall be a will-o'-the-wisp."[13] Such a view depends wholly on the belief that there is a supernatural Power, all-good and all-righteous, who has created a powerful universe. The ground for such belief, to sum it up in a word, is *faith*; yet faith in most of its forms is a proposition that disregards the need of empirical verification. All that we really know about the universe as such is that it has existed from eternity with its laws and atomic configurations for no discernible purpose. Purpose is a local episodic event in the universe. Human actions are purposive, yes, but cosmic purpose, should there be one, goes beyond what we know.

Man is mortal, he is part of the perishing events. Not only individuals, but the race and the very earth which is our abode will perish. How, then, shall we meet death? Life being transitory, its brief duration should be cherished as much as possible. However transitory life may be, it is the only source of value in the world; a world without life would be a world without value. Although life is a transient event, we need not be obsessed with this prospect. Awareness of our mortality is inescapable, but this awareness need not weaken our desire to live. The present has intrinsic value, and we can live a good life without other-worldly consolation.

And though we cannot with triumph say that death is swallowed up in victory, we can face it with fortitude. As Norbert Wiener says, "In a very real sense we are shipwrecked passengers on a doomed planet. Yet even in a shipwreck, human decencies and human values do not necessarily vanish, and we must make the most of them. We shall go down, but let it be

---

12 *Philosophical Theology*, London, Cambridge U Pre, 1956, Vol. II, p. 272.
13 *Ibid.*, p. 272.

in a manner to which we may look forward as worthy of our dignity."[14]

Finally, we can hope and act for a vicarious immortality. All men are mortal, yet some have attained a degree of immortality. The immortals of the human race—Plato, Buddha, Jesus, Newton, Shakespeare, Beethoven, and many others—live in our gratitude. To the extent that we contribute something that human beings can value we too will achieve some degree of immortality. As individuals we are born, grow up, become old and die, but the race will go on as long as the earth endures. As members of the human race we can have a more generous conception of life than the self-centered one of the past.

We have not created the world, and we have to take the world as we find it. There is no evidence that the world is governed by an omnipotent, beneficient God and that ultimately all is for the best, nor is there evidence for what the pessimists maintain, that all is for the worst. Both good and evil exist. Through the sources of power that are available in our natural world we may increase the good and diminish the evil.

---

14 *The Human Use of Human Beings,* Boston, H M., 1954, p. 40.

INDEX